WHAT PEOPLE ARE SAYING ABOUT

I AM BOU...

"I Love this Book! Ilie Cioara's ... ... goes beyond Mystical literature, it is Experier... ...erature. *I Am Boundlessness* is a collection of poetry and prose that actually transports the reader into the Experience of what is written. The Book itself is Boundless.

It is a journey into the Boundless Emptiness where Pure Aliveness is Directly Experienced. It must be experienced by the reader, all words fail to describe it, you must simply read it and in doing so you will become it.

Ilie Cioara can be compared to just a few: Rumi, Tolle, but he actually is beyond what they have written in his simplicity of explanation and the experience of the poetry puts him in a category by himself."
Lee Petersen, The Way of Consciousness Radio Show

"This work stands independently of ancient traditions, well known sages, and the current nonduality scene. That is refreshing. This, and Cioara's other works, are among the finest books on nondual consciousness.

Hearing the words of Ilie Cioara, the mind like a clever curtain lifts, the small ego drops, and the silent choir of boundlessness is known as Self. His way is to invite lucid attention to the activity of the mind."
Jerry Katz, Nonduality.com

"*I Am Boundlessness* by the gifted Self Realised Mystic and Poet Ilie Cioara is indeed a precious gift for all those embarking on the great spiritual adventure of endeavouring to wake up from the dread sleep of samsara.

This distinguished author broadly follows the teachings of the great Sage, Sri Bhagavan Ramana Maharshi, and also has affinities with Eckhart Tolle and J. Krishnamurti. His brief Essays are written in an attractive poetic style with clarity and wisdom. They are obviously based on experience rather than scholastic book knowledge. I would strongly recommend this precious book to all those aspirants who are interested in and working for Self Realisation."
Alan Jacobs, President of the Ramana Maharshi Foundation UK

"The Light of Consciousness that comes through Ilie Cioara's truly inspired words in this work is both illuminating and transformative. Page after page, Cioara reveals – through poetry and prose – the deeper dimension within us all and how we are empowered by recognizing or knowing our oneness with Infinite Boundlessness, while yet engaging in the mundane activities of our daily life.

This is a "spirit-guide" that the reader will benefit most from if he or she savors each line, each verse and each paragraph."
Peter Stafford Sumner, The Seer

"Best book out there to date on direct experience for those weary of belief and philosophical statements that can't be lived."
Jody Breeck, Indiana, USA

"*I Am Boundlessness* is one of those very rare books that carry the potent energy of Truth itself. The simple act of reading the words themselves usher in a profound transmission of peace and joy and sacredness that drives deep into the soul. Just as the light of a candle can easily be transferred into the next candle, so this deep, profound Truth that is expressed in this work, is transmitted straight into the heart.

Reading this book is like a communion with the highest essence of Life itself. Actually, this book is so energetically potent

that just holding the book in your hands, without reading a word will offer a glimpse of this beautiful Reality that Ilie so poetically speaks of. This truly is a must for anyone who seeks to experience the boundless Love and Light that is the essence of us all."
Rosemary Cochran, California, USA

"Cioara tells us over and over that seeing the truth for ourselves is all that counts. He asks us to simply use these words to cross the gap and then to let them fall and melt away like snowflakes on warm ground. It's good advice. If you are looking for a bridge, look no further. It is in your hand right now.

Ilie Cioara sings like an angel, calling us Home; his heart is on every page. Ilie's poetry actually guides us toward that Light. It is beautiful, lyrical, and deeply moving. Petrica Verdes is a gifted translator and an artist; he paints with the master's words and his canvas is spaciousness itself."
Fred Davis, Awakening Clarity

"I have read all of the English translations of Ilie Cioara's books, but *I Am Boundlessness* strikes a special chord with its presentation of the essential movement of Self-knowing through the redirection of Attention to what is.

This book, through its verse and prose sections, takes the reader on a practical "tour" of Self-knowing, showing us precisely what we can expect to find – notwithstanding the limitations of words and the conceptual – and, most importantly, what our individual responsibility is in this endeavour of transforming our ontological perspective from that of limitedness to one of boundlessness.

In every attentive reading, the mystery jumps at you, threatening to devour you whole so that only the unlimited remains.

Do not read this book if you want to remain as you are."
Professor Kriben Pilay, Noumenon Journal

"This is the third book by Ilie Cioara that I have had the privilege of reading. The title in itself *I Am Boundlessness* reflects the nature and transformative power contained within.

Once again he connects us to our infinite and eternal state of being with such an ease of mind that we are left only with the words: Thank You!"

Charles Bergeron, Maine, USA

Ilie Cioara website thesilencebook.blogspot.com

I Am
Boundlessness

Ilie Cioara

I Am
Boundlessness

BOOKS

Winchester, UK
Washington, USA

First published by O-Books, 2012
O-Books is an imprint of John Hunt Publishing Ltd., Laurel House, Station Approach,
Alresford, Hants, SO24 9JH, UK
office1@jhpbooks.net
www.johnhuntpublishing.com

For distributor details and how to order please visit the 'Ordering' section on our website.

Text copyright: Ilie Cioara, Petrica Verdes 2011

thesilencebook.blogspot.com

ISBN: 978 1 78099 197 9

A CIP catalogue record for this book is available from the British Library.

Translation by Petrica Verdes

Design: Lee Nash

Printed in the UK by CPI Antony Rowe

We operate a distinctive and ethical publishing philosophy in all
areas of our business, from our global network of authors to
production and worldwide distribution.

CONTENTS

Introduction

The encounter with ourselves I am trying to describe in this book is the result of personal experience. Each human being has access to this reality.

Lucid, all-encompassing Attention is the only instrument we use in order to encounter the mechanical reactions of our mind. We need to specify that this is not an attention directed by will, pursuing a certain purpose or goal, but it is that Attention which ensues spontaneously, by itself, when a noise or a thought, an image, a desire or fear appears on the surface of our consciousness. All-encompassing and all-illuminating, it dissipates everything that appears on the mirror of the mind, without leaving any memory residues.

In that moment of "psychological emptiness", the notion of "me" disappears and, in the unity of our being, we are integrated into the Great Whole. Let us also mention that Attention is the manifestation of the Sacred within us – "our divine Nature"; by enlightening the mind, It dispels and dissipates all darkness and It unites us with Divinity for a split second.

A truly healthy mind functions only when it is needed. The rest of the time, it must be silent. From this silence or peace all benedictions ensue: spiritual and physical. In that instantaneous moment of stillness of the mind, the "ego" loses its energies, as well as its intrinsic fictitious importance. The physical body functions perfectly, unhindered by chaotic and stressful thoughts, which cause psychological turmoil and fragment our energy.

Intuitive understanding is another important element in the practice of "Self-knowing". When the mind is silent, through the spontaneous enlightenment of lucid Attention, the divine Spark within our being guides us through intuitive impulses, solving any life problem we encounter in the happiest way possible.

In any circumstances of Life we might find ourselves, let us never resort to compromises regarding the objective truth! Let us never resort to a cloak of lies, in order to camouflage the absolute reality of Truth.

Life in Its movement, newness from one moment to another, is our best teacher and master, for It lays before us a series of events and phenomena that we have to address and encounter. As disciples of Life, how do we respond? We simply avoid or reject these events; we oppose or run away from them.

In fact, all the events that Life lays before us in Its eternal movement are meant to benefit and teach us. Our duty is to respond with an impersonal action. Let us, therefore, immediately fulfill precisely what Life requests of us in that particular moment, without being hindered by our personal goals or agendas, selfish by their very nature.

Finally, "Self-knowing" also requires something else of us: inner serenity, a fundamental and indispensable condition. We can attain this beneficial harmony no matter what our circumstances may be; all we need to do is ask ourselves: Am I Whole, here and now – body, mind and spirit? In this circumstance as well, the Light-Attention helps us realize the integrity of our being.

Another essential factor in the process of "Knowing" is the "ego", the "personal self", the personality or the surface consciousness. In fact, this "ego" is not an independent entity, with a well-determined content and essence; rather it only fulfills certain functions of manifestation within the human being.

Therefore, the "ego" thinks, imagines, judges, assesses, analyzes, accumulates and stores information, knowledge and experiences. It conditions and deconditions us; it stores a large number of memories, and through repetition these memories become permanent. Because of this fiction, the human being becomes a prisoner of what he remembers, knows or possesses.

The "ego" represents the human being's false nature; it was born out of an erroneous interpretation when the individual became identified with his somatic structure, with the mind and its whole memory content.

Because of this erroneous interpretation, a person's entire activity unfolds within a limited perspective of extreme egocentrism. "I know", "I possess", "I have" and "I want to be" guides his entire activity, from birth until he takes his last breath. The "ego" cannot do anything without a well-defined goal or purpose; its center of interest is its true god, directing all its actions.

The human being is born with certain inclinations and aptitudes, which influenced his existence throughout the long succession of incarnations. The whole past from countless millennia is written in the individual's "ego". Therefore, within each man lie various qualities and attitudes: for instance, the toughness of the stone, the cunning of the fox, the greediness of the wolf and the ferociousness of the lion. In man, these attitudes are even more exacerbated. In fact, man's cruelty far surpasses that of savage animals. Animals kill only in order to feed themselves, compelled by their organic necessities. Why does man kill? Cannibalism was practiced in very distant ancient times. Nevertheless, the hatred, violence and murder perpetrated by man against man has continued and continues in our so-called cultured and civilized world. Can a sane mind find any rational justification for all the large-scale wars in which, directly or indirectly, almost the whole of humanity participates?

Who is responsible for the conflicts between states or alliances of states? Does the fault lie in the leaders, hungry for glory and fame?! The leaders are nothing but the creation of the masses of citizens. Each member of that nation contributed to the emergence of the leader, through their purely egoic energies. The moral quality of the ruler of a country can only be the creation of each citizen's attitude.

This "ego" is characterized by ceaseless chaotic activity, creating a psychological climate which attracts all the misfortunes that befall a certain region of the planet or a country. Ambition, greed, lies, dishonesty, arrogance, pride and hatred are so frequently encountered in the daily life of each individual that they are considered to be natural, normal attitudes.

All these human deficiencies have been mentioned since ancient times; naturally, a vast range of practices have been devised in order to eliminate them. But all such attempts have failed. There is no need to bring arguments in this regard. A simple overall glance at what we see around us, in our daily collective environment, extended to the level of the geographical region or country and also, generally, on the entire surface of the planet... and the evidence speaks for itself.

Religions, as well as other practices – each promising but not delivering – demonstrate through themselves that they have not created beneficial moral changes, compared to the ancient world. On the contrary, religions, with their different dogmas and rituals, separate and create even further enmity between human beings. The same effects can be noticed when we examine the various philosophical theories and practices, each offering the same deceptive promise of transforming the human psyche. All of these have created nothing more than external masks; our contemporaries have managed to hide their inner ugliness better than their ancient ancestors.

We ask ourselves today, seeing these undeniable results before our very eyes, as facts speak for themselves: What is the fundamental mistake of their approach?

All individuals who follow a religious faith or any other type of practice try to realize their being with the help of the mind or the "ego". Yet, the mind cannot radically transform itself. All it can do is create mere superficial changes, a deceptive appearance. In this manner, the practitioner creates a protective mask, carefully hiding his inner ugliness. This psychosomatic mask is nothing but a further degradation: that of hypocrisy.

"Self-knowing" is not a faith, nor is it a method to be practiced by pursuing a certain result, goal, purpose or ideal. As we have shown from the very beginning, the practice of "Knowing" starts from "what is", namely the apparition on the mirror of the mind of: thoughts, images, desires etc. – in one word: all the manifestations of the "ego". Encountering them with the flame of Light-Attention leads to their disappearance.

In the simplicity of this encounter, the memory residues – which brought us into the present incarnation – disappear. This phenomenon finally leads to the state of Liberation and to the integration of the human being.

In order to better understand this simple encounter with ourselves, let us remember that the "ego" is closely connected to desire. Therefore, there is no "ego" without desire, and no desire without the "ego". The very source of the "ego" is desire, taking many forms and facets, one more cunning than the other. Let us also point out that there is no such thing as a holy desire, as some would have us believe. This is why: no matter what its object might be, each desire hides fear in its shadow. Fear of failure, for instance, of not being good enough, of losing what we possess.

But fear and holiness are two separate dimensions. The presence of one completely excludes the other.

In order to encounter the Absolute Truth, let us also mention that this Truth is indivisible. The fragment of Truth existent within us has the characteristics of the Whole, from which it was never separated or detached. Only by encountering the Truth can the practitioner radically transform the imperfection characteristic of the human being in a state of "personal self".

Therefore, this simple encounter with "our divine Nature" is also a beneficial-transformative action – devoid of any form of wanting, search or imagination.

Do not be content with mere intellectual understanding, for it is relative and absolutely detrimental, as it only fortifies the authority of the "ego". Persistently and diligently try to realize the intuitive understanding that the verse merely points to – through a direct, personal experience, by eliminating the memory baggage or the presence of the author.

Ilie Cioara

Uniqueness

I am here as well as everywhere in the Immense Infinite,
I permeate everything.
All is within Me, I Am present in All,
There is nothing outside of Me, seen or unseen.

I have no cause and no Source of creation,
I have always been and I will always be, endlessly,
For what has no beginning will have no end,
In Essence and form, I Am a perfect Whole.

Uniqueness – as Unity – encompasses all,
It is within each of us, eternally revealing itself,
Effort or will are meaningless,
Both are forms of struggle, creating stress and turmoil.

The mind and its structure is but a fragment,
Unable to encompass the independent Sublime:
Uniqueness, in its natural Greatness,
Existent in the Aliveness of Life, manifest Joy.

***

Therefore, the mind must be silent, in humbleness,
In this silence – the being is spontaneously fulfilled;
Body and mind together – a perfect melting,
Discover the Beauty of Life in Its sacred flow.

All is accomplished through "real Knowing",
Living with what is in the present moment;
A perfect melting, in perfect Oneness,
A total Uniqueness – eternal freshness.

Attention is the accompanying Light,
Its intrinsic value is similar to the Sun,
Dissipating darkness, illusions and anomalies,
Offering priceless jewels of Joy.

Uniqueness is, by its very nature, pure Simplicity; it is the greatest discovery made by the master of this planet, the human being.

This Uniqueness or Primordial Energy is everywhere and in everything, seen or unseen, perceived or unperceived by the human senses. It has always existed and it will always exist, eternally. Therefore, It has no creator separate from Its own existence. It is unlimited and boundless; we can also call It Immensity, encompassing the Whole Existence. Its Center is everywhere and nowhere in particular.

It is Stillness on the exterior – for It is extended into Infinity – and in the interior It is eternal movement, an infinite diversity of forms and manifestations, encompassing all, from forms of gross matter to human beings, the most elevated. Similarly, from galaxies and universes, billions of light years away – the macrocosmos – to the small infinite – the microcosmos – all forms of individual existence have the ability, independence and potential to evolve on the scale of evolution, the immensity of the Divine Body, awaiting for Its children to return home.

Therefore, all forms of life within the Uniqueness are in perpetual movement and constant evolution, from the most rudimentary to the most subtle.

After this quick overall perspective, let us return to us, human beings; this Uniqueness lies within us as well, as a simple "luminous dot", with similar characteristics to the Immense all-encompassing Whole. This is, in fact, the Spirit existent within each human being, revealing Itself by Itself, without any need for will, effort, struggle or imagination, for they only create tensional states and turmoil.

The mind as a whole is just a fragment of the incarnated being, unable to encompass the independent Sublime, that Divine Spark with all-encompassing powers, endowing us with the State of Pure Happiness.

Therefore, by using our mind – no matter how knowledgeable – there is no chance of encountering the Absolute Truth, Wisdom or Happiness! The knowing mind must be silent! Only when it is silent, in humbleness, it is endowed with a priceless quality, an incredible spiritual advantage; all this occurs spontaneously, in a flash.

When the mind is silent, body and Spirit become One, in a perfect melting. In this context, the individual functions as a Whole, able to discover the Beauty of Life and to live moments of supreme Joy, fueled by the State of Being Itself, in the eternal moment Here and Now.

If correctly applied, "Self-knowing" leads the practitioner to this wonderful fulfillment, by coming into contact and detaching from the eternal Uniqueness, manifested in unfolding moments. The succession of moments in perpetual renewal requires that the experiencer employ all his unused neuro-cerebral potential in order to correctly understand the intrinsic freshness of the movement of the Aliveness. For only a new mind is able to truly perceive, understand and live the Beauty of Life.

The only instrument necessary in order to experience this phenomenon is lucid, all-encompassing Attention. It is like a sun or a laser; by Its simple presence, all darkness disappears.

Therefore, Attention – a quality of the Sacred within us – dispels, dissolves and shatters any thoughts, images, desires, fears etc. which appear on the mirror of consciousness as reactions of the mind to the encounter with the Eternal Now. This Moment – Uniqueness – has no past and will have no future. The unconditional disappearance of these intruders, barging into the present, will naturally and spontaneously provide the priceless advantages of our encounter with the Sublime Truth.

Nothingness

Nothingness is the non-form, the nothing, nonexistence,
It is also the Void of the mind – Infinite Existence,
It includes and permeates All that exists in the Universe,
It has no limits, no bounds.

After the seventh level of consciousness, we become only
What Is,
Boundless in its totality, thinking becomes Immensity.
This is the Nothingness, holding everything together
in orbit,
Planets and galaxies, all matter and forms.

Therefore, from now on, all is just simple Being,
The threshold of the Whole Eternity with Boundless
thinking.
A thought can be placed anywhere, in a flash:
On the Moon, the Sun or any galaxy, spontaneously.

The state of Being – a State of Godliness,
We are Oneness with God, we are eternal Love,
Moment to moment, intertwined with emotion.
This is the potential of every human being.

"Self-knowing", through natural being,
Is the simplest Path towards this real experience,
Encountering the deceptive, mechanical mind,
With the light of Attention.

The right encounter instantly dissipates it,
In the "psychological emptiness", the new Man appears,
Affirming his existence as sublime action:
Joy and Happiness, integrated as One.

Never accept that this simplicity is difficult!
Only the "ego" affirms this, not the Sacredness
Of our own Being, as creative will,
Constant intelligence in perpetual change.

Nothingness is the void, nonexistence, the nothing, the non-thing. Simultaneously, It is also the Infinite, the Existence which permeates All that exists in the Boundless Universe. It has no limits, therefore it is Boundlessness.

Each time we realize the State of Being, we also experience Boundless Thinking, which is, in fact, the same Immensity we can also call Nothingness. This Nothingness holds all the planets, stars, galaxies and universes in orbit, as well as all their content.

Therefore, in a simple state of No-mind we encounter the eternal State of Being, which is, in fact, the Infinite Energy or God. Practically, we are in a state of Boundless Thinking; in a split second we can place a Thought on the Moon, the Sun or any galaxy.

When we truly encounter the State of Being through personal experience, we realize our Godliness, for in that sublime Moment we and God are in a perfect communion, manifested as eternal Love.

Therefore, each of us – woman or man – is endowed with this natural functional capacity. It is attained with the help of lucid and all-encompassing Attention, which instantly dissipates the mechanism of the delusive, illusory mind. As soon as this "Psychological Void" or Peace of the Soul appears, the New Man affirms his existence and sublime behavior as unconditional Love, Joy and Happiness, free from any external motivations.

Never affirm that the fulfillment of simplicity is difficult! Such a foolish statement belongs to the degraded

"ego" and not to the Sacredness of being that We Are,
endowed with creative will and constant Intelligence in
perpetual change.

I Am Boundlessness

I am spontaneous simplicity,
Mind, heart and feeling,
A whole being, absolute fullness,
Love in action.

This state
Reveals itself naturally;
When the mind is awakened,
All becomes One.

The past melts away
In the light of all-encompassing Attention;
In emptiness, the Sacred reveals itself
In its natural brilliance.

Experiencing the moment,
The personal mind is dissipated,
Expanding into Infinity
As Universal Mind.

Each such encounter
Transforms us radically,
For in each sparkle of consciousness
We are newness, Divinity, Reality!

Detachment from Words

The word is just a symbol, its meaning is limited,
An association of images, created by man, throughout time.
It has a certain sense, in verbal communication,
Buried in estimations and mental conclusions.

It is never reality, only a product of time,
Creating duality and obscuring the brightness of life.
Through programmed confusion, the limited "ego"
Ceaselessly repeats itself, in thought and speech.

The detachment from words carries within itself
                        the whole mystery,
In such a state, Truth is revealed.
The individual is liberated, lucid and attentive,
                        in movement,
He is not a slave of words, he is silence in action.

By silently watching the reaction to the word,
It immediately disappears and in its ineffable climate
A precious integration ensues – a priceless light –
Dissipating all darkness – man fulfills his being.

When the individual is not a slave of the mental residue:
                        the word,
He is in a direct relationship, moving without thoughts;
In an all-encompassing embrace, the "self" is dissolved
By the integral being, pulsating ceaselessly.

In such a state, all he encounters – he understands,
He can describe and explain, according to its law,
He uses words to express
This true, real and alive experience to others.

The spoken or written word represents, among others, the usual means of communication between human beings in the dimension of the known.

Words are mere symbols, endowed with certain meanings. Their sense is chosen by convention, yet their value is always relative, as they can never express reality in itself, the essence of a fact. No matter how broad their sense, they are nevertheless limited, especially when they try to express something beyond the limited dimension.

The word is not only unable to express reality, but it also represents a hindrance, obstructing the direct experience of Life. For this reason, it is absolutely necessary to detach from any words.

An instrument of mental expression, the word is used in the limited realm of knowledge. It is undeniably useful within this dimension. Nevertheless, beyond the limited, it can never have access to the Infinite, no matter how broad its content of expression.

Only by being detached from words are we able to come into direct contact with Truth, with Reality, in a state of bliss.

The word is noise and limitedness; through its automatisms, it creates confusion and conflictual states, preventing us from encountering Love, harmony, living in a state beyond time and space.

When thinking is silent, words also disappear, for thoughts affirm their existence in the form of words.

Let us try – each for himself – for each of us has the potential to realize this mysterious detachment; without it, it is impossible to encounter Eternity.

First of all, we must exclude any desire, purpose, ideal or goal from the very start. This beginning is absolutely essential in order to correctly make this experiment. Any prior motivation is nothing but a mental projection, part of the limited dimension.

Therefore, free of purpose, motives or goals, we simply observe the wandering of the mind. We just listen and watch, with our full attention, any desire, emotion, image, the whole cerebral activity, without creating any conversations in our head.

This direct contact – in its simplicity – effortlessly ends

the entire movement. Thus, the mind is empty of its whole content in the span of the moment. In this flash of consciousness, it becomes completely inactive, able to encounter the new, the Boundless.

The emptiness of the mind attained in this indirect and totally disinterested manner can be called the state of meditation and the beginning of "Self-knowing". In this state, we detach from the old and melt with the new, with the ceaseless movement of the Aliveness.

On the great journey of knowing oneself, we set off as a being free from the past and we end the encounter just as free from the moment we have just experienced.

The new appears spontaneously in the mirror of our soul, in a perfect state of equilibrium; we express it in simple words, easy to understand by everyone.

The Unknown

What is not, what does not exist, the mysterious Unknown,
So controversial, it is impossible to see or foresee it
With our narrow mind; we cannot approach it or
                                        demonstrate it
Through images, thoughts and speech.

It is an eternal mystery, we can never encompass or
comprehend it
With our miserable "ego", living in the past;
The Unknown appears as a lightning bolt, evident through
itself,
Like lightning it disappears, in the flash of the moment.

In the following moment, it becomes the "known",
For it has already become old, as the revelation vanishes;
Time devours all, through the consumed present,
Each event becomes old, as the moment dies.

Encountering the freshness in movement, we need to
be innocence,
A clear spirit and an acute perception;
Thus, the past disappears, effortlessly,
Liberated in the moment, the new man appears,
spontaneously.

Absolute purity and elevating Love,
He is a splendid light, eternally beneficial;
Each moment is an opportunity for integration,
Preparing the State of Enlightenment.

The Unknown is also called: God, Reality, the Absolute,
Boundlessness, Cosmic Energy, the Great Whole, the
Absolute Truth, Stillness etc. These are mere symbols and
do not represent reality in itself. They are just a vague
attempt to express something that the ordinary mind
cannot comprehend. In this circumstance, the mere

utterance of these words is an impiety, a lack of respect. For how could a mind closed within its small shell comprehend boundless Stillness without beginning and without end?!

It cannot, and when, nevertheless, it tries to do so, it is out of ignorance, misunderstanding or arrogance.

This Absolute Reality is everywhere as well as within the essence of all things, seen or unseen; it is also within each human being. Its very existence within us provides us with the ability to perfect ourselves and to experience happiness without cause.

All human beings have the capacity to discover the Unknown. None of us is excluded from this wonderful opportunity. It depends on us and on us alone to explore the depth of our being, in order to bring this precious treasure to light. Of course, it is hard, difficult work and it requires certain sacrifices.

We reach the Source of life by peeling off the confused, chaotic and sticky layers of the surface consciousness. Only by demolishing the ego – this idol we worship and bow to every day – does the path towards the greatness of the Skies open.

It is only when this egoistic structure sees its power-lessness and becomes silent, in humbleness, that the "psychological emptiness" ensues naturally and Eternity is revealed. It comes to us, by Itself, because the walls which enclosed us in our small-minded universe suddenly collapse in the sparkling flash of consciousness.

The moment experienced in this manner becomes the known; immediately, it becomes old, as time devours all that occurs in the present moment. Each event or happening, alive in the moment, becomes old as soon as the moment is consumed.

In order to encounter the constant newness of life in

movement, we need to welcome it with a clear, innocent mind, free from any memory baggage. Attention is the flame bringing light into the darkest corners of consciousness, by consuming and burning the whole past preserved in the memory, which created the man trapped in time-space.

As the conditioned man disappears, a new man is born, with a limitless mind, absolute purity and Creative Love. This is the Divinity within us, revealing Itself, by Itself, when we become humble, by realizing how our own small-mindedness is holding us prisoner at the level of the "ego".

In conclusion, as we have discovered the great mystery of the Unknown, each moment becomes a wonderful opportunity to become integrated into the Great Cosmic Energy, leading to the State of Enlightenment.

Therefore, let us not miss the present moment. It depends only on us to make this wise choice.

Moving Stillness

These two words, an apparent paradox,
Express a true reality;
It is a description of Divinity in Its endless being,
Absolute Existence, greatness and immensity.

It is in All and Everything, seen or unseen,
In the Immense Boundlessness, existing as unknown,
Its boundary is the Infinite, therefore It has the attribute
of Stillness,
As there is no space to extend Its limitlessness.

In Its interior, there is constant movement,
Nowhere is there stagnation or frozenness,
From rock to human being. In all that exists,
All is in perpetual transformation, manifest as movement.

Therefore Divinity
Reveals Its existence, united with the whole,
As Moving Stillness – an undeniable Truth,
Offering each of us Beauty and True Life.

Do not search for it on the outside, but always
within yourself,
It is the Essence of your being, always available;
The path is short, the road is straight – experiencing
freedom
As well as Love and the gem of Happiness.

We start from "Being Here and Now", in total silence,
Accepting, without complaining, all that the flow of Life
brings in Its real movement,
Good or bad, together, are in fact gifts from the divine,
Through them, we know who we are – as reactions of
the human mind.

Everything we encounter spontaneously – disappears in
a flash,
Liberated from time, we are creative beings;
One with Life, we manifest ourselves as Love.
There is no other path towards the Sacred Perfection.

This name, one of many given to the Absolute Truth – an unnatural combination of two linguistic symbols which apparently exclude each other – is not a paradox. It explains the supreme Reality – in an absolute and undeniable way. This Cosmic Energy is everywhere and in everything – seen or unseen – extended into Infinity. In Its limitless span, It becomes Stillness, as there is no space around It to allow a further extension. The boundlessness of the Infinite endows It with the attribute of Stillness.

On the other hand, in the Immense interior of this reality there is permanent movement. Nowhere in this Universe is there any fixedness: in the mineral, vegetal and animal realms. As such, from the granite rock – which is only apparently dead – to the human being, everything is in constant movement.

Therefore, Divinity reveals Its undeniable existence through this attribute as perpetual mobility, as Movement and Stillness, as eternal Truth, easy to experience and verify by any human being.

Let us not search for It outside our being, but start the investigation, each time, in our interior. We can discover Its Reality through the shortest and quickest way possible, by searching each time in the center of our being. In the peace, order, harmony and independence of our being, we find the time and the place to discover Sacredness. This extra-ordinary simplicity will certainly make you distrustful. Be attentive! Do not listen to the superficial labeling of your mind. The mind is only a fragment of our being, whose effects we experience as gnashing of teeth and curses, trapped in a vengeful "ego".

No effort or anything of the kind is needed in order to accomplish this blissful encounter with the Moving Stillness. Just try to be present, "Here and Now"! With the help of Light-Attention, you become whole, in a state of "Being". In this state, we accept everything that Life brings in its movement as permanent newness, pleasant or unpleasant surprises, or even disastrous ones.

If we see all these and accept them as they come, we are in a state of creation, in permanent Union with Divinity. In this blissful melting with the Whole, we are boundless Love; through Its simple presence, It dispels any hardship or succession of difficult events we might eventually experience in our life.

Discovering the Truth

In order to discover the new, appearing in a flash,
Always freshness, in endless movement,
Do we need anything else? Anything outside ourselves?
Or does Reality reveal Itself in simplicity, directly?

The great mystery is right in front of our eyes, requesting
that we discover It
Each for himself! And finally we unite with It.
The moment is the unique reality, it must not be missed,
Attention is its essence – listening and watching.

Thoughts, desires, images, barging in as reactions,
An all-encompassing observation of their natural effects:
Some cause pleasure, some cause pain,
We don't have any options or choices.

Totally impartial, we just come into contact with "what is",
Neither past nor future weave their story;
Thinking is completely mute, there are no expectations,
No such thing as purpose or goal.

Therefore, we become a "void" of infinite proportions,
Able to receive the holy truths;
They come and are reflected in the mirror of our being,
Without any anticipation or desired consequences.

When the Truth is revealed, it becomes old, instantly,
For it becomes "known", a true obstacle
To encountering the new moment, in its eternal flow,
The Universe is freshness in perpetual vibration.

Integrated into the Sacredness of the moment –
                              an undeniable Truth,
We melt into It, without needing to search for It;
Happy, we fully live limitless Love,
This is the great fulfillment, existent within each of us.

When "someone" claims that he knows what truth is, he is either ignorant, or an imposter, or simply a victim of his own imagination. The following undeniable facts prove the impossibility of any prior knowledge of the Absolute Truth.

Truth is an eternal mystery, revealing its reality, by Itself, simultaneously with the flow of the moment.

What do we need to do or not do, practically, in order to encounter Truth?

Is there a path we can follow, searching for this mysterious revelation?

Not at all! We can only search for something when we have a prior knowledge of what we are searching for. Since it is impossible to initiate a real search in order to find It – let us allow Truth to find us. This is what we need to do, as "Self-knowing":

With the help of all-encompassing Attention, each practitioner listens to and watches the movements of the mind, reacting mechanically to the challenges of life, without pursuing any results. We encounter both pleasant and painful events – brought forth by the encounter with the movements of the Aliveness – in the same manner, without any choices.

This simple encounter with the memory impulses – illuminated by the rays of Attention – makes them disappear spontaneously. Simultaneously, our whole being becomes an infinite "emptiness" or a state of "Pure

Consciousness". This is the fortunate moment when Truth reveals Itself, enveloping our whole being.

As Truth is revealed, It immediately becomes old. It becomes known and, as such, it is an obstacle to the encounter with the next unfolding moment. The newness of this moment becomes old and outdated the next moment. Therefore, we must let it go, so that the freshness of our being can encounter the eternal newness of Truth, in close connection with the eternal flow of time, measured through the flash of the moment.

In this state, we live moments of real Love, and the true meaning of our life as beings caught in the cycle of reincarnation is fulfilled. This realization is written in each human being's destiny. Accelerating or postponing this fortunate event depends on our personal power and diligence.

The very fact that you have come across this knowledge is a sign that you have already reached a level of spiritual maturity, enabling you to practice "Self-knowing", "here and now".

Silence

Silence, stillness, peace – a priceless treasure,
Integrates our being, as an infinite structure;
When it is truly experienced, it transforms us,
Time, which enslaved us, disappears spontaneously.

There are no signs, traces left, such as images, memories,
The moment silence appears, it opens the path for Love;
It is the foundation of meditation and a timeless
                                              fulfillment,
With no support in thinking or ideal formulas.

Noise and turmoil do not disturb or oppose it,
For they are completely separate dimensions;
Silence is boundless, one with Immensity,
Noise is created in time, it is confined and limited.

A cultivated silence, attained through effort,
Is not a pure silence, nor a true support.
The "ego" is unable – through its activity –
To attain this state, free from duality.

Silence appears spontaneously when noise is understood,
Watching and listening, without any goal or purpose;
Attention is the priceless instrument
Encountering the pointless movement of the
                                    confused "self".

Therefore, beloved reader, silence is not to be sought,
But only noise needs to be understood, in utter simplicity.
A direct contact with it dissipates it without fail,
In the "emptiness" that ensues, peace affirms itself,
                                              by itself.

When the noise dimension of the small "ego"
Ceases to be, through this simple watching,
A new dimension, expanding into Boundlessness,
Is present by itself – the being melts into It.

Joy, Happiness and creative Love
Are attained naturally, through this simple encounter,
Accessible to anyone who wants to understand
One's being and to encounter silence.

The peace of the soul, silence, the "void" or "psychological emptiness", the stillness or passiveness of the mind represents the priceless climate leading to the integration of our being into Infinity. In this state, time and space disappear; the egoistic limitedness of the "personal self" is transformed and its authority is shattered.

Silence is not a product of thought or imagination, as a mental projection or as an ideal to pursue. The noise of words and, generally, any turmoil do not oppose or come into conflict with silence, because they exist in distinct, separate dimensions. Silence is boundless, limitless, whereas noise is confined to the time-space dimension.

Direct experience proves to us that a silence achieved through sustained efforts of will is not a pure silence. Such a forced silence can never be of any real and beneficial help, because, through its activity, the "ego" is never able to attain true silence – completely free of duality.

Practically, silence appears naturally and spontaneously the moment noise and its movement are enveloped with an all-encompassing perception and understood through the simplicity of listening. Lucid Attention is the only instrument necessary in the encounter with the pointless movement of the chaotic, confused "self".

In conclusion, silence need not be sought; instead, we need to perceive, understand and dissipate the noise existent in the present moment. In the "emptiness" that ensues when noise disappears, silence envelops our being, as a natural phenomenon, transcending our whole being into Boundlessness. Simultaneously with this blissful encounter, we discover – through a direct experience – creative Love, Kindness and Happiness, free from any time-space motivations.

Each individual who is determined and seriously interested in discovering the true meaning of existence as an incarnated being has access to this experiment of "Knowing" one's own being. By overcoming the limited "self", we are integrated into the Great Whole.

I Am That I Am

I was and I am, what I have always been,
A beginning without beginning,
From Eternity to Eternity
In an unmoving "Now", continuously regenerated.

I was and I am endless Perfection,
Sacredness re-created – moment to moment,
The Boundless Aliveness – in constant evolution
As a sacred fulfillment.

Does the Boundlessness of these words baffle you?
Leave your mind aside, if you want to experience
These hallowing invitations with me,
For only thus can you encounter the Sacred sparkles.

You are a Spark, a part of Me, Sacred Essence,
I and you are "One" – a perfect union,
Constant freshness – an integrated structure,
We are Aliveness – as a real experience.

There is no other way to encounter Me,
Only by being Unity, in Sublime Harmony,
The expansion of "Self-knowing",
When we become the Whole – Unlimited – Immense!

We are Pure Consciousness, in the moment,
Without any prior purpose or effort,
Created by the vicious "ego", pursuing a goal,
Always egocentric, small-minded and confused.

The all-encompassing, lucid, watchful Attention
Offers us clarity and holy harmony;
Thus you reach Me, in your innocent nature,
And the whole being becomes Joy.

From now on, you are "One" with Me – a Universal Whole,
Illuminated each moment, simply being in the present;
By creating and re-creating, each moment,
The Sublime is more Sublime, constantly and perpetually.

In this subject, the Divinity within me, permeating all and everything, addresses my self and the reader, trying to prove Its Existence, which comes from Eternity and moves towards the same Eternity.

The perpetually renewing "Now" is what connects that which was in the past to what will be in the mysterious future. Each movement of the Immense Aliveness is a process of creation and re-creation, an evolution towards more elevated forms.

In order to understand me, That Who I Am, as well as yourself, for you are the same as me, you need to leave your mind aside, as it is and it will always remain a limited structure, unable to embrace and comprehend Boundlessness. You and I are Sparks detached from the Immense Flame of the Great Whole – the entire Limitlessness from which everything originates and to which everything returns, that is, the Source of all Sources, of all and everything, seen or unseen.

In order to correctly understand It, we recommend "Self-knowing" – not just conceptually – but through a direct experience of the actual phenomenon, in which we become What We truly Are, the perpetually creative Divine.

Encountering the Whole is attained in a state of "Being Here and Now", as Pure Consciousness in moments perpetually unfolding and flowing towards Eternity. The practice of "direct Knowing" is attained without any effort or struggle, in the absence of the "ego". We do not pursue any goals and there are no expectations of a certain result.

This fullness, ensuing spontaneously, confirms – by itself and through itself – the power of the correct practice, an experience of Oneness with the Great Universal Whole. Simultaneously, Harmony, Love, Beauty, Kindness and boundless Joy appear as a perfect bouquet – expressing themselves, through themselves, as holy and hallowing energies.

In this sublime context, Perfection eternally perfects itself on the ascending path towards more subtle forms, with similar qualities to the Greatness of the Infinite.

Bring Your "Ego" to the Light!

Bring your "ego" to the light,
In complete freedom,
For it defines itself
When it encounters Life.

The "ego" is the fruit of yesterday,
Searching for pleasure and satisfaction,
Rejecting what it dislikes,
Constantly and obsessively.

By simply becoming conscious of it,
Its energy is dissipated,
With each encounter,
It is weakened and loses its hold.

In this state,
It becomes a shadow,
Finally it vanishes, perishes,
Annulled by integration.

From now on, Love is present,
As an intrinsic law;
Through It, the being is creative,
A Sacred transformation.

With the Light-Attention,
We experience full consciousness,
Man as Divinity,
In natural simplicity.

The ordinary man, conditioned by a misguided education, lives and acts as a true prisoner on the level of the egocentric "personal self". This fictitious structure, created by the past and the future, can never encounter the beauty and reality of Life in permanent mobility and freshness in the sparkle of the moment. Relying on an outdated past and an uncertain future, this imaginary entity behaves as if handicapped.

How can we dispel its incapacity, obstructing the true understanding of Life? The title is relevant. It was suggested by Antal, our astral guide, during one of the spiritual sessions. The great teacher urged us to bring this "I" to the light; it exposes itself and arises on the surface of our consciousness as we encounter the challenges of Life. We need not do anything except encounter it with the flame of Attention, each time it appears – as a reaction of the mind.

Its principal characteristic is turmoil. Agitation sustains, feeds and fortifies its existence. The "ego" is always terrified by the passiveness of the mind or the peace of the soul. In those moments, it loses its energy and its decisional authority. Created by the "yesterday" and the thousands of "yesterdays", the "I" searches for what is a source of pleasure and satisfaction and avoids, escapes or opposes what it dislikes. In the light of Attention it is simply dissipated, as well as the energies which sustain and create its existence. This direct contact weakens its force and finally makes it disappear, by depleting its dysfunctional energies.

Breaking the shell in which the "ego" keeps us prisoners is a mysterious phenomenon. We do not know when it will happen. It depends on the thickness of the walls of our prison, as well as on the determination of the individual who has truly understood the importance of "Self-knowing". Any attempt to fight with the "ego" can only fortify its structure and deepen its roots on the astral plane. Simultaneously with the phenomenon of Liberation, Love appears, leading our whole being and guiding us through intuitive impulses.

Opinion and the Truth

The opinion is a hollow thought, lacking content,
Created by the intellect, based on the past,
Fueled by the mass of mental residues,
Crystalizing the ego and its small-minded values.

It is always limited and conflictual,
Through its personal nature, it creates disagreement.
As many "egos", as many opinions – according to
                                        conditioning,
The past creates the opinion and its subjective meaning.

Truth, in Its essence, is completely different,
Through It, the human being is psychologically absorbed
                                        into Infinity,
Face to face with "what is" – in perfect simplicity,
We experience the Sacred Truth and Its reality.

Only in the silence of the mind, Truth completely takes
                                        over our being,
When time and space disappear in the
                    "memory emptiness";
We all see Truth the same way – without any difference,
It reveals Itself through Itself, as a natural effect.

Opinion, point of view, concept, idea or belief – all of these are nothing but hollow thoughts, devoid of content. It is nothing but an intellectual creation based on images extracted from the mass of memory residues.

Initiating an opinion – as well as its whole content – in fact crystalizes the activity of the "personal self" and its relative, petty values.

Because any opinion is personal, limited and uncertain, it is also conflictual; each time, it will confront itself with other opinions, according to the subjective perception of the individual.

There are as many opinions as there are people on this Earth – functioning as "egos", as separate entities, created by conditioning.

***

The Absolute Truth is completely different in Its essence. It is completely independent from memory accumulations. Therefore, it is not influenced by science or culture. Created through Itself, by Itself, it has no beginning and no end. Its existence is continuous and It is manifest eternally as Perfection.

All human beings who experience this Truth perceive it as uniqueness. In fact, in the boundless Universe, only Truth can affirm "I Am". We can also call it: God, Primordial Energy, the Source of all Sources etc.

There is only one way to encounter it: when the individual mind becomes silent, in humbleness, as it has understood its powerlessness, then and only then – in the Peace of the soul – Truth reveals Itself as existent within us as well as everywhere in the Universe. In other words: in this "psychological void", the Divinity existent within us reveals the Divinity existent in all that is in the immense

Boundlessness.

The mind of the experiencer becomes silent as it is illuminated by the flame of lucid, all-encompassing Attention.

What Is

In the whole Universe, nothing is static,
Everything is in perpetual movement:
Either movement in time-space, perceived by the senses,
Or inner, hidden movement – such as, for instance,
within a rock.

The moment is the hand of the clock, witnessing
everything
Through movement and stillness,
Or "Being" and "Not Being" – as Unity;
It appears in a flash, it is in fact Reality.

In order to understand What Is – the Absolute Truth,
Unique Reality in its essence and content,
We start from what this united Wholeness "is not",
From a part of It, as fragmentation.

"Self-knowing" is the beginning of this experiment,
And not the other way around, as some mistakenly affirm;
Therefore, by knowing What We Are not, we encounter
                                                    Reality,
Intrinsic existence – One with Divinity.

                              ***

To facilitate understanding, let us explain further:
God is "All That Is", as well as "What Is not"
                    (the deceitful appearance),
We are exactly the same, wholeness and fragmentation
Re-creating the Whole – the Sublime essence.

We are neither the body, nor the mind, nor the memories,
Nor glory, titles, fame, attachments, feelings;
We are beyond all these,
We are more than all these – we are Eternity

Without beginning or end, as Nothingness and Everything;
This experiment demonstrates that the Whole,
Present "Here and Now", in the moment,
Is an Everlasting Eternity, existent unto Itself.

Nowhere in the Immense Universe is there any state of
fixedness or immobility, even in places where our senses
perceive everything as static, for instance, in a rock. Its
reality is completely different. It has been scientifically
proven that gross matter is, in fact, energy, and energy is
in permanent movement, and movement in itself is Life.
Therefore, the rock also had a beginning and is undergoing

a process of evolution, on the return journey to where it originated, in a past spanning billions of years.

Therefore, the Aliveness in permanent-renewing movement lies in all forms of existence: mineral, vegetal and animal. Each movement of the Aliveness takes two aspects: being and non-being, in a state of unity. In order to understand the existential Whole, we start from Its part, from the fragment.

"Self-knowing" is the starting point for each experiment, and not the other way around, as the conditioned mind mistakenly believes. Only by knowing what we are not, such as: thought, image, desire, fear etc. can we encounter the Reality of our being as intrinsic Existence – One with Divinity. In other words: God is everything that exists in the Boundless Universe, as well as what does not exist, namely the ever-changing appearance.

The individual is the same: by understanding the fragment, we discover the whole. Therefore, we are neither the body, nor the mind with its vast range of memories we are attached and give importance to. Beyond all this, we truly are Eternity, without beginning and without end. We are Nothingness and Everything. This is, in fact, the experience which proves the Whole in Its eternal greatness, "Here and Now", as absolute newness, in eternal unfoldment.

Conditioning

Since the first years of our existence as newly embodied Souls, we were trapped into various educational and moral patterns by the family or the social environment into which we were born. Parents, teachers and educators only offered us what they themselves had inherited from the previous generations. In this manner, our minds were shaped, encountering the newness and freshness of Life – in Its eternal unfoldment – through uncontrollable mechanical reactions.

At the basis of this education, the selfish and fearful personal self-interest has been implanted from the very beginning. Shaped by and relying on this foundation, we will never be able to truly understand our Divine Nature, nor the Divine Nature of our fellow beings as well as that of our whole environment.

We can easily assess the results of this erroneous education from its effects, affecting our relationships with our fellow beings, as well as with the rest of the world. An attentive and objective glance, as a simple observer, reveals that the whole tragedy of this world – so obvious in its conflictual states, contradictions and tensions, with disastrous effects on the individual and on society – has its source in this misguided education.

The beginning of the new millennium requires that humanity resort to a new way of approaching Life in Its general unfoldment. Technically, there has been a huge qualitative leap – a century ago, not even the most imaginative mind could have foreseen or imagined it; whereas morally and spiritually, the inhabitants of planet Earth still live in a profound state of primitivism.

Therefore, the state of development achieved in the external world brings awareness to the fact that we need to do something – something different from anything we have done up to now – regarding our inner world. "Self-knowing" is available to everyone; each human being is able to apply it, regardless of the circumstances of one's existence. It is neither a theory, nor a method, nor is it a religious faith – all of these are accompanied by a series of interdictions, demands and obligations imposed on the individual.

"Knowing" is an authentic response to the movement and newness of Life, requesting that we give It our full attention, in order to completely understand It and live It, to the benefit of the individual and the society. Let us remember, therefore, when encountering Life, that we need to give It all our respect and attention. And we cannot do this unless we are a whole man, with a new mind, fresh from one moment to another.

The old man, based on hollow images – shadows of the past – barging into the present in the form of mental reactions, represents an unsurpassable obstacle to encountering and understanding the newness brought forth by the movement of Life. Therefore, the only problem that needs to be solved is the old man, with his obsessive and confusing reactions.

Everything disappears spontaneously by simply becoming aware of this unwelcome intruder. To put it another way: we are a simple observer or witness, who only watches everything that appears on the screen of our consciousness. As the false disappears, peace, harmony and a total independence of the Soul ensue.

In this "emptiness" or "psychological void", our being is united as a functional Whole, in an eternal present to present – as a state of "Being" or Pure Consciousness, in which unconditional Love is manifest; in Oneness with the creative Sublime, we create a New Man, through a qualitative leap on the scale of evolution.

The Roots of Will Lie in the "Ego"

The roots of will lie in the "ego",
In this hotbed, passions and terrible traumas are born;
Man is enslaved by them, he acts mechanically,
His whole life becomes a dysfunctional psychosis.

By its very nature, will is practically violence,
Effort defines it, fueled by persistence;
The harder the effort, the tougher the "ego" becomes,
Degrading the human being, feeding his fictitious
                                         self-importance.

Psychologically, will creates permanent conflict
Between the real and the unreal, mind becomes even more
                                         confused.
All the aggression in the world is born out of this error,
Through excesses of will, violence proliferates.

If the "ego" disappears, the root of will vanishes,
We live in timelessness, in perfect harmony;
Everything we encounter, we solve in simplicity,
Life itself provides the solution, through Its reality.

Therefore, watching – attentively – each movement of
the "ego" as will,
Enveloped in silence, it is dissipated,
In its place, the being is illuminated by the Sacred present
within,
One with Reality – the divine Greatness.

Let us ask the question: What is will?
We give it an exaggerated importance and we often take pride in it.

Will is a psychological function by which consciousness pursues a certain goal. We can also describe it as "desire in action".

Where are the roots of will? Who initiates it and fuels it with energy, in order to fulfill its goal?

The roots of will lie in our surface consciousness or the "personal self". Here, in this fictitious structure, lies the source of all human passions and vanities. Enslaved and led by them, the human being becomes a mere mechanism, weaving the cloth of life each moment.

The nature of will is violence!

Are you surprised by this description? Let us dispel any doubts.

In the field of consciousness, a thought that we dislike appears. What do we do each time? With the help of will we try to either chase it away or cover it with another thought, deemed as pleasant or useful. This act of will appears as a desire, which tries – through violence – to eliminate the first impulse in order to take its place. In reality, will is nothing but a struggle between two desires.

What are the immediate consequences? First of all, our being is divided by this conflictual state and pointless waste of energy. The sustained effort of will – through its intensity and toughness – degrades the being who aspires to realization.

On a psychological level, will generates perpetual conflictual states between what is real, in the moment, and the unreal imaginary purpose we want to achieve in an unpredictable future.

The general aggressiveness encountered in all walks of life originates in the individual will.

What happens when this "ego" which degrades our being – divine in its essence – disappears?

With its disappearance, the fragmentary energies and characteristics which sustain its fictitious structure will also disappear. As the "ego" vanishes, we will encounter the state of timelessness; we will function as Oneness, in perfect order and harmony. From that moment on, everything Life brings in our path is solved in perfect simplicity.

Therefore, point your full attention to everything that appears in the field of consciousness as "ego" or will. The simple encounter with the humble silence of the mind makes them disappear, without any intervention on our part. From now on, the whole being is illuminated by the Sacred – present within each of us – uniting us with the One Reality, where we live and experience bliss as a state of Pure Consciousness, in the climate of divine greatness.

The State of "Being"

The simple state of "being" is a creative state,
Through it, the being is in harmony, each
                                    renewing moment;
We see, listen and understand, through a
                                    different perception,
All that Life brings in its flow – fresh, never
                                    encountered before.

It is an eternal mystery, time does not influence it,
When encountered correctly, the human being is
                                    integrated.
In this state, mind and body are unity,
A timeless structure, part of Eternity.

There are no problems, no conflicts, no contradictions,
Everything is dissipated, without any consequences;
The purity of the encounter clears the confusion:
The conditioned mind and its painful nature.

It is truly impossible to encounter "what is"
As long as we exist as an ephemeral, possessive "self";
It is a real obstacle, always obstructing
And obscuring the wonder of Life, through its
                                    small-minded fiction.

First of all, it needs to be dissolved – nothing is left of it,
Not even a faint shadow, intervening as an impulse.
Through understanding, the "ego" disappears,
                              humble and powerless,
Seeing its inability to encounter the beauty.

Without "self", the whole being is extended into Infinity,
We encompass everything we encounter perfectly,
The newness of being melts into the newness of Life,
A perfect communion, free from duality.

Without this union, nothing can be accomplished,
All is deceit if we are not integrated
Into "what is", what appears, brought by the movement
                                        of Life,
In a harmonious order, changing each moment.

The simple state of Pure Consciousness or the state of "being", in its purity, is a holy fulfillment. It provides us with peace, harmony and inner aloneness. It enables us to commune with Life, transforming and renewing us each moment.

In this simplicity, man – as a complete being, present to present – sees, listens and understands everything that Life brings in Its eternal freshness. The flow of the Aliveness in perpetual unfoldment, defined as Eternity, is an eternal mystery.

If this mysterious Energy is encountered in a state of "being", what else do we notice?

In perfect union, our being – body, mind and spirit – becomes "One". As a complete being, we experience the state of timelessness and we are naturally and spontaneously united with Eternity.

In this state, all contradictions, conflictual states, fears, doubts or problems disappear without any intervention on our part. In fact, the purity of this encounter cleanses, burns, melts and dissipates the whole conditioned mind, fearful and confusing, stressful and painful by its very nature.

Be aware nevertheless! Do not try to attain this state of "being" with the help of the ephemeral "ego" or "personal self". This fiction is a true obstacle – in fact, the only obstacle – always interfering and interposing itself between us and Life, like a dense shadow, preventing any practical experience and encounter with Reality.

Seeing this impediment, we have no other alternative than its complete dissolution. The "ego" disappears spontaneously when illuminated by the rays of all-encompassing Attention. In that moment, it becomes humbly silent, seeing its inability to encounter Divinity, manifest in all and everything that exists as all-inclusive and all-pervading eternity and beauty.

When this fiction is absent, our united being expands into Infinity; everything we encounter, we encompass and understand in a perfect way. From now on – as a new being – we encounter the newness of Life in a perfect communion. Without this intrinsic melting with Life, we cannot accomplish anything durable as an incarnated being, attracted by our own destiny in order to cleanse the dross of our worldly past.

Only in the integration of our being can we eliminate all the deceitful states that the practitioners of methods and faiths wrongly deem as true accomplishments.

Non-action

Non-action is a state of stillness,
When all movement is absent;
It is not an opinion, created by thought,
A false assessment, in its confined limitedness.

In the whole Universe, as an intrinsic law,
There is stillness and movement, quick as a flash
                                        of lightning or slow.
In its essence, movement is life – perpetual transformation,
The old form ascending to higher forms of evolution.

Without evolution, there would be fixedness and darkness,
Difficult to imagine or describe in words.
The state of non-action is helpful in thinking,
For it is, in itself, an action, clearing the mind.

The mind is non-active when it detaches from the past,
For the old is the death of the newly-born newness,
                                        in the now.
When the past is spontaneously silent, there is
                                no movement,
A sublime peace descends upon us – the mind is lucid
                                        and clear.

It observes, listens and learns, and detaches again,
Always encountering the moment directly, without
looking back;
By pursuing this path, the human being is transformed,
Without purpose, effort or will.

Only in the quiet mind, Truth is revealed
Through non-action.
The whole being is wide open
As energy-purity, expanding into the Infinite.

In the dimension of knowledge, always trapped within the limited confines of its own content, it is a common belief that the only way to achieve a result is through a certain action, directed by the individual's psychosomatic energy.

First we project the thing we want to achieve and then we progressively attempt to attain it through ceaseless efforts, fueled by a well-trained will.

From the very start, we distinguish: the projection of the goal, self-interest and the action pursuing the achievement. All these are initiated and led – under the influence of a prior knowledge – by the individual as an "ego" conditioned by the time and space he developed in, physically and mentally.

From the very first step we take, we already know the final goal or object, and we endow it with utmost importance. The instruments we use in order to attain this purpose or ideal are: imagination, permanent strain, fueled by the act of will and by self-interest.

In the spiritual realm, in pursuit of the ennoblement of the human soul, things are completely different. Here, will, imagination, self-interest and effort only further amplify egocentrism, subtly degrading our being. The psychological ugliness which surfaces automatically from the interior of our being is carefully hidden under various beautiful masks. In this manner, the practitioner forges a fictitious surface existence, deeming it as spiritual progress. In fact, it is nothing but an "ego", deceiving itself and also trying to deceive the external world.

This is what humanity has been doing since very ancient times. It is an attempt to radically transform the aberrant and possessive "ego", by using the very means of the "ego".

It was and continues to be a wrong path; this is proven both by the troubled past of humanity, as well as by the present pettiness of the individual and of society as a whole. The human interrelations are nothing but reactions, conditioned by self-interests, egoistic by their very nature. The contradictions, conflicts, fears, ambition and hatred encountered in the inner world of the individual are also externalized in the outside world, with disastrous consequences.

The human being has become so degraded that the so-called religious man's search for God has become an excuse for interminable disputes and arguments, violent confrontations, often degenerating into bloody wars.

If the activity of the mind – which makes up the "ego" – a creation of time – cannot create a radical transformation within itself, how else can we approach this problem?

We need to do the opposite of what moral and educational systems have done and continue to do, pursuing changes in the dysfunctional behavior of the individual.

Therefore, we will approach the ennoblement of the human soul through the silence of the mind, of the thinking process, of the "ego" in all its manifestations. This categorical inactivity – we call it "Non-action".

It is easy to understand theoretically and intellectually. How can we attain it practically, in spite of the chaotic and mechanical impulses which rule our lives?

In order to attain an authentic experience, we will use all-encompassing, clear and lucid Attention as an instrument of transformation. With It, we simply come into a direct, spontaneous and disinterested contact with each attempt of movement on the part of the mind, such as thoughts, images, desires, fears etc.

This direct relationship with ourselves as we are, in that very moment, will certainly dissolve and dissipate everything that appears as a psychological movement. In this manner, we liberate ourselves from the relative energies of the "ego". In the "psychological emptiness" which ensues naturally, our being is integrated into non-dimension, in union with the Universal Mind.

A correct practice of this encounter with ourselves creates the effects we mentioned earlier, without any need to anticipate their attainment.

Humbleness

It is not a creation of thought, a method of taming
                                        human nature,
Trapped in formulas of acceptance and submission,
Following a certain purpose, in a certain context.
It cannot be planted and cultivated like a flower,
It cannot be nurtured so it can grow, in time.

All these pursuits are futile self-deceit,
The "ego" lives in hope and it becomes more arrogant.
Humbleness in itself is meaningless,
Based on superstition and belief, it chains human beings.

Detached from thought, humbleness is a real experience,
The past is silent, all is enveloped in peace,
In the state of "nothingness", there is no big or small.
Humbleness has no connection with the past,
We learn from "not knowing", without the need
                                        for teachers.

Embracing the new, the human being expands into Infinity,
He dies to the past and is reborn as "not knowing",
Perfectly embracing life.

The true state of humbleness is not something we conceive and attain within the confines of the "ego" structure; its accomplishments are and will always remain relative.

Being humble does not mean submitting ourselves unconditionally to a spiritual authority and automatically executing whatever that authority tells us to do or not to do.

The state of humility does not mean training ourselves to follow external patterns of behavior, achieved through study or repetition, as second nature, such as we encounter in monastic practices.

It is not a model, or a form of adaptation to a certain pattern. Imitating a spiritual authority can only degrade us. The behavior of the imitator – regardless of who he imitates – is nothing but a mask. The life of such an imitator is detached from reality. He constantly tries to adjust this mask, which is in contradiction to the natural impulses and reactions of his being.

Humbleness cannot be cultivated, as we would a garden flower. It cannot appear as a result of memory or habit, performed over a period of time. It does not increase or decrease, like the level of a river. Either it truly exists, and in this case it is complete, whole, or it is completely missing.

The true state of humbleness appears by itself, spontaneously, as soon as thinking has ceased any activity. In this climate of equilibrium and inner harmony, the personality disappears. We are just a true psychological "nothing". It is a state of lucid attention – an all-encompassing super-consciousness, in which there is no purpose, motive or goal. Only by reaching this state can we investigate, learn and discover, through understanding, the true newness of life, ever-changing from one moment to another.

This wonderful "psychological void" or inactivity of the mind enables the Infinite within us to integrate our whole being into the Great Whole, to which – by our very origin – we belong completely.

Cause and Effect

In all things, seen or unseen,
From the smallest atoms
To the stars and the immense galaxies,
All is ruled by the intrinsic Law of cause and effect.

The oak already exists in the acorn, the sun in an electron;
In mud, rock, leaf of grass, insect, elephant and man,
The same Law rules – as a pre-established order,
In feelings, thoughts and deeds.

Dominated by our ancestral causes,
Yesterday and the thousands of yesterdays we have
                                    lived unconsciously
Created the reality of our "ego",
Imposing itself through old residues.

The chaos present today in the world belongs to the old,
If we don't dissolve it, the effect of today
Will become the cause of tomorrow,
Increasing our state of chaos.

How can we break the chain and end the evil?
Only in one way:
When we watch, attentively, wholly and persistently
All reactions as effects to Life's challenges.

The past which enslaved us disappears,
The human being is free – a state of Enlightenment,
Detached from causality – he is creative force
And absolute Love with hallowing effects.

In the wholeness and boundlessness of Existence, in all things seen and unseen – from the subparticles of the atom to the immense galaxies – all is interrelated through cause and effect. The Law of Cause and Effect rules everywhere and everything in the immense Universe.

Just as a majestic oak tree lies within an acorn, a sun is temporarily enclosed within an electron. In a clod of mud, a rock, a leaf of grass, an insect, an elephant or a human being rules one and the same Law of Interdependency, as a pre-established order.

Each individual's specific mentality, made up of thoughts, feelings and facts, clearly demonstrates the dominant influence of ancestral causes. Past lives, as well as our personal past from this incarnation, demonstrate our existence as chained "egos". The chaos, confusion and misery – so obvious in the world of today – are a natural outcome, manifested through automatisms of the mind, as an effect of these causes.

We are all able to know our current level of moral evolution. Each moment reveals the man, a creation of time, incarnated in order to expiate the mistakes and karma he created at some point in the past. Be attentive to the reactions of your mind! They show us who we really are.

If these reactions-effects are not encountered in the right manner, they will become generating causes of another destiny, and we will have to inevitably return to Earth in order to expiate it.

The chain of reincarnation breaks when the reactions and the causes are dissipated. Life's challenges are a wonderful opportunity to know ourselves, and all-encompassing Attention is the only instrument – perpetually available to us – able to shatter the reactions of the ancestral mind.

Finally, the disappearance of these effects and of their sustaining causes will lead to the state of Liberation. The countless series of incarnations comes to an end. The divine Spark returns to the Source where it originated, in order to fulfill the lengthy experiment in association with various forms of manifestation within the Infinite.

Self-healing

It is possible to heal oneself without medicines,
Without healers and energetic healing
Transmitted as impulse-thoughts to the vital body,
Which permeates the physical – as an integrated whole.

Such self-healing has always existed,
Man is his own doctor, perpetually healing himself,
Body and mind united with the Sublime,
Functioning as one.

Here is my invitation to a real, practical experience,
Apply this, as soon as you have the opportunity,
In your daily existence – as incarnated "egos",
As your destiny, to expiate your karma.

In my early life – I experienced fear, stress,
Years spent in a harsh labor camp,
All these affected my physical health,
Through frequent shocks my heart was weakened,
Foretelling an imminent heart attack.

Frequent states of dizziness, nausea,
My pulse was arrhythmic,
My physical body damaged, out of balance;
I accepted that death was imminent –
I was eighty-three years old at the time.

Suddenly, an intuitive impulse from the depth of my being,
Like a healing flash of light,
Operated without any intervention on my part,
Leaving everything in the hands of the Sacred.

***

I lay down on the bed, in complete relaxation,
My eyes were closed, my mind silent, in total acceptance,
My whole being was open to the Divine Energy –
An innocent thought, filled with joy:

"Let thy will be done! I surrender completely,
If not, allow me to complete
The message of 'Self-knowing' – blissful integration,
Offered by your Grace, for the entire world!"

***

In my profound silence, here is what followed:
Like an arrow – a burning fire enveloped my heart,
The impact was painless – a clear sign of healing,
My heart started to regenerate.

The next day, I surrendered again,
Without any invocation – just a pure detachment
From my mind and from the worldly – a perfect silence;
Its effects felt like the attentive caress of a hand.

Two years have passed – my heart feels renewed,
It gives no signs of the old past,
The sharp painful effects
Of many decades of living in stress.

Within each man lies the essence of the Universe,
Molecules and atoms make up the physical body,
As well as Pure Essence and its transformative powers,
Healing and repairing any deficiencies.

Physically and spiritually, "Self-knowing" provides
Inner means of healing and Sacred wholeness;
Everyone can experience this – manifested as Love,
United with Divinity – as a Supreme Fulfillment.

Intuition

An innate ability of profound contemplation,
Existent in every human being, revealing itself in silence;
Through it, we have access to the sacred Reality,
We see the Absolute Truth as It is.

Through intuition, Spirit affirms Itself.
Any error is excluded!
It has no connection to the knowing mind,
Based on accumulations and past experiences.

Intuition affirms itself as a lightning-like impulse,
As a flash, guiding and inviting us
To follow a certain path and solve conflicts,
Which cannot be solved by ordinary means.

It barges into consciousness in a moment of silence
And it immediately disappears – without leaving any echo;
We ask ourselves no questions, we do not analyze,
All these are useless, they increase confusion.

Mind, in its nature, conditioned by time,
Strays us from the path revealed by Spirit,
Which often appears to be irrational;
By relying on arguments, the individual falls into a trap.

Mind with its reasons is always old and outdated,
Whereas Life's surprises are perpetual newness,
The only way to understand and resolve them
Is by listening to the Soul – in constant contact with It.

Let us, therefore, enter Its realm,
Perfectly attentive, we watch the poverty of the mind,
In silent humbleness. Let us listen, totally,
To the subtle intuitions, saving us from trouble,
And follow their guidance.

Intuition is a quality of the soul, accessible to each human being, regardless of one's intellectual capacity. Lengthy experience has proven a logical, rational fact: when the mind is too burdened by memory accumulations, it obstructs the onset of Intuition. Because Intuition appears only in the "emptiness" of the mind, this phenomenon is difficult to attain when our intellectual ability dominates us overbearingly, as knowledge barges into the alive, active present of the movement of Life.

It is only when the mind is silent that the Soul provides the unique solution, solving any problem concerning our existence in the most fortunate manner.

Does the mind become silent by simply wishing or ordering it to be silent? Not at all! If we nevertheless attempt to silence it by means of concentration, we do not attain true peace, but only a state of tension – which is, in fact, also a state of the mind – and not an experience of harmony or inner relaxation or total independence.

In order to attain this inner silence, we use the flame of Attention; by simply enlightening the reactions of the mind, It makes them disappear spontaneously. In the "psychological emptiness" that ensues, all that remains is the Essence of our being – the Divine Spark as a state of Pure Consciousness. In that moment of profound harmony, Spirit conveys to us directly what we need to do.

The flash of Intuition disappears spontaneously, without leaving any echoes or reactions. We do not make any comments regarding Its guidance, but we apply it straight away.

Be aware, nevertheless, because shortly afterwards we will receive a new suggestion, this time provided by the "ego". Its advice comes much more slowly, and the curious part is that it is supported by arguments, which lead us into error. Caught in the traps of the "ego" or the knowing mind, we will realize immediately that we have missed the divine guidance. In other words, we betray the Divine and listen to the confused and aberrant worldliness of the obtuse, petty and deceitful mind.

Therefore, in order to encounter the permanent newness of Life, as well as Its wise guidance, we need to be a Whole Man – led by the Soul and not by the knowing mind; for it is, by its very nature, old, based on previous experiences, whose apparition in the present overshadows clear vision and the direct contact with the Aliveness in Its unfoldment.

Let us therefore remain in the depth of our being, in the Divine realm, in contact with the Essence of our being, as much as possible, perfectly attentive to the poverty and humbleness of the mind. Let us listen to the intuitive impulses, without hesitation. In this context we will never err, and a state of permanent joy will permeate our whole life.

Bliss

The intellect will never be able
To elevate the individual to superior realms,
To perfect harmony – transforming our life,
Full of hate and conflict – laying the foundation of Love.

No matter how cultured,
It will never be capable of transformation.
In the realm of the mind, truth is nothing but ashes,
Only the pure Truth can burn the ugliness and impurity
in man.

The state of bliss unfolds into Infinity,
It cannot be cultivated or nurtured, like a plant,
By the absurd, chained "self",
Always seeking to fulfill its fragmentary pleasure.

It does not come through images or desires,
Neither through will, nor as a reward to a prayer;
When desire is egoistic in its endeavors,
Man creates his limits and is chained by them.

If you search the whole Earth, you cannot encounter it,
It is a priceless treasure, beyond all value;
All the gold, pearls and diamonds in the world
Could not pay for it!

A true elixir, revealing the meaning of Life,
It ensues naturally, as an immense Light,
When the "ego" is completely silent, the being transcends,
In contact with Boundlessness – absorbed into Eternity.

The whole secret lies in silence, the holy peace within,
It ensues spontaneously, when we watch the turmoil.
In a state of integration, the human being is superhuman,
Fulfilling his potential, on the path towards the Supreme.

Bliss is a state of complete happiness, free from any cause
or motivation. It cannot be planted or cultivated, such as a
flower, by the self-interested "ego", in any circumstance. It
cannot be the fruit of imagination, nor can it be attained

through persistent effort or will. It cannot be negotiated, for it is priceless.

No prayers – no matter how persistent and passionate – can help us attain it, for all these are nothing but egoistic endeavors, whose author is none other than the "personal self", always pursuing its self-interest. Its activity cannot go beyond the dimension and the limits of its time-space structure.

This bliss or boundless Happiness ensues spontaneously, as soon as the ego becomes humble and silent, as it has understood its powerlessness. In the unforced and undesired silence, any ideal, goal or purpose is completely absent and our being expands into Infinity. In a state of truly Pure Energy, we are perfectly conscious of an immense joy, united with Eternity.

Every human being who has understood – through a direct experience – the great mystery of inner harmony and equilibrium has access to this holy fulfillment. Each reaction of the mind is a wonderful opportunity to attain the state of bliss. Try to encounter the movement of the "ego" right now, in this very moment. The flame of Attention dissipates it instantly, and your being is integrated, in union with the Sublime. Do not content yourselves with a mere intellectual understanding of the phenomenon!

Only a perfect encounter with the chaotic movement of the mind creates the beneficial effects we mentioned earlier. Your perseverance and diligence will not remain unrewarded. It is definitely worth it! The blessings of spiritual fulfillment are greater than any benedictions the most fantastic human mind can imagine.

True Love

We can never experience and encounter it
                     through thinking,
It is an eternal mystery, of infinite dimensions;
It appears spontaneously in the "psychological emptiness",
When the "ego" and its content is completely shattered.

In this state, Sacred Love appears,
Absolute newness with transformative effects;
It offers us beauty, boundless happiness,
Without motivations, completely empty of images.

We encounter the "psychological void" through
                           "Self-knowing",
Attentive, we just watch "what is" and we integrate into it.
When the surface is silent, the depth affirms itself,
As a Sublime Energy – unwanted, unsought.

In silence – the humble mind becomes Universal,
The only way of being – as timelessness;
Only in this simplicity, we discover the Sublime Treasure,
For millennia it has been awaiting to reveal itself.

The word "love" has become a dull cliché, because it is used too often as a mere formula, devoid of content and meaning. The family egoism provides countless examples in this regard. The attachment of the mother for her child causes her to commit some of the most terrible deeds in order to protect her offspring.

Marriages out of so-called love – in reality based on sensuality – are another frequent example. In this case as well, the outcome is woeful. Shortly after the contract between the two souls has been signed, jealousy, arguments, often hatred followed by separation are a natural outcome.

In both cases, the initial attitude and its effects are natural consequences, because everything takes place within the limited structure of the "personal self" or the "ego".

True Love cannot be encountered – in any circumstance – within the sphere of the intellect or the surface consciousness. The ordinary mind cannot encompass it, for It is an eternal mystery and an integral part of the sphere of Infinity.

If this is the case, what do we need to do?

It is very simple: the mind must be silent!

Does it become silent if we order it to? Of course not!

Can we force silence with the help of efforts of will?

This is not an efficient solution either; any such activity only divides the same mind into two antagonistic fragments.

The silence or passiveness of the mind can only be attained with the help of lucid, spontaneous and all-encompassing Attention.

This simple encounter with the flashes of Attention dissolves the reactions of the mind. In the "psychological void" that appears, we discover the state of timelessness and we melt into Universality.

In this happy state we know – through direct experience – boundless Love, in which the entity who loves has completely disappeared. We are purely and simply Love, enveloping all and everything, without any choices.

Such an experiencer creates radical changes, ennobling his whole being, creating similar effects on the entire humankind.

Life Is Change

Life in Its Essence is a real Process of permanent change,
Life is as It Is, as It affirms Itself – free of conditioning.
We can call it God or Absolute Existence,
Through Itself Eternity – of Infinite proportions.

Therefore God is eternal change, in Its natural movement,
Constantly re-creating Itself through Its divine power;
It is also Energy in constant change, constant becoming,
Free from desires.

Truth is the same – another word which defines It,
"That Which Is the Way It Is" – right Now, in this moment,
Affirming Itself through Itself;
Therefore, It is change, permanent transformation,
Perpetual being and Suchness.

***

Coming back to us, human beings,
Overwhelmed by circumstances, interpreted by the
                                    human mind;
Let us ask this question: Can we live without conditioning,
Just as Life, God, Truth is – unfolding in the moment?

Does it seem difficult? Not at all! Nothing needs to
                                    be done!
Concentration, effort, struggle are meaningless,
Through them, we will never attain the state of Liberation
And Enlightenment, as independent beings.

On the contrary, when the "ego" uses such means,
Pursuing a purpose or goal,
We become even more conditioned and chained,
Unable to comprehend Life in Its unfoldment.

Simply try this experience – as an individual conditioned
                                    by time:
Just watch all this turmoil with a lucid Attention,
It immediately disappears, for it is made of ephemeral
                                    thoughts
Without any consistency; you were identified with them.

From now on, as a liberated man, you live a different
experience,
Past, present and future become one single movement,
Re-creating our Whole being,
One with Reality – a Creative Energy.

The Aliveness as Essence of Life is in a permanent Process of change, in moments unfolding eternally as newness, freshness each second. Life, in Its wholeness and complexity, Is as It Is – unconditioned by anything or anyone. We can call it God or Absolute Existence, by Itself and through Itself, spanning into Infinity and defined as such.

Therefore, God is eternal change in Its natural movement of creation and re-creation. It is Infinite Energy – existent everywhere and in everything – and It needs nothing, for everything within It unfolds naturally.

The Absolute Truth is another name used by human beings to define the presence of What Is as It Is, "Here and Now", in this very moment, affirming Itself by Itself.

After these overall statements regarding the title, let us return to us, human beings, involved daily in the ceaseless Process of Life. Let us ask ourselves: Is it possible to live unconditionally, such as Life, God, Truth is, unfolding perpetually?! Do you find the question inappropriate, or the actual practice difficult, as a personal experience?

No activity of the mind, such as effort, struggle, concentration, repeating formulas etc. is necessary. The activity of the mind is unable to create harmony, peace, silence or the liberation from the chains of the "ego". On the contrary! By using the instruments of the "personal self", we strengthen the conditioning of the old, ignorant, fearful and possessive man even further. This is what the human race has been doing for thousands of years, and the results are obvious in their negativity.

"Direct Knowing" provides accessible solutions to each individual who is discontent with his manner of functioning in the encounter with daily Life. By its very simplicity, this experiment is met with mistrust at first; as we progress, the "ego" itself, sensing that its existence is endangered, tries to demoralize us and to convince us not to trust this practice.

Here is how we can engage, with our whole being, on the path of spiritual perfection: with the help of Light-Attention we encounter the reactions of the mind, triggered by the perpetual challenges of Life. The simplicity of the encounter with these reactions makes them disappear spontaneously. In the "emptiness" that ensues, our being becomes Whole – body, mind and Spirit as One. This wholeness, in the eternal moment "Here and Now", creates and re-creates our universal being, in communion with the Great Energy or the wholeness of Life – in Its eternal Process of becoming.

The Universal Man

The universal man is within each of us,
Awaiting to reveal himself, through spontaneous
                                        integration;
It all depends on us – becoming free from the ancestral
                                        bondage,
From our ancient shell: the conflictual "ego".

"Psychological Emptiness" is the gate to Boundlessness,
One with It, spontaneously, we expand;
Love and Wisdom are our constant companions,
Through them, we are happiness and creative being.

The leap to a New Era is attained through Love,
Man overcomes his nature – integrated into the Universe.
Practically, the starting point is our obsessive thinking,
This degrading structure needs to be dissolved.

It is dissipated, vanishes, when we encounter it attentively,
A new man appears, and a new life,
Free from duality and conflictual states,
Constantly integrated into the present moment.

This universal man lies within each human being, awaiting to be discovered through personal investigation. He is: Love, Beauty, Kindness and Intelligence; these are attributes of his uniqueness.

He is equally manifest in a scholar or in an ordinary man, rich or poor, leader or the led, master or disciple. Discovering this blissful Reality depends on each individual; It manifests Itself spontaneously, simultaneously with the sacrifice of the surface consciousness of the "self" or the ancestral "ego".

With an all-encompassing Attention, we encounter each reaction of the mind triggered by the challenges of Life. A simple and direct contact with these reactions dissipates them and, in the "emptiness" that ensues, the mind expands to Infinity, melting with Immensity.

In this lightning-like sparkle we become a universal man

and we affirm ourselves as Love and intuitive Intelligence. The scholar or the scientist who attains this blissful state will use his discoveries in the physical world only in a way that is beneficial to the whole of humankind. The rich man will open his heart and his purse in order to help those who are in need. The ordinary man – experiencing the same fortunate phenomenon – will be an example of honest work and fair relationships with his fellow beings.

This moral and spiritual qualitative leap to a new era can only be attained through a radical transformation of the individual. This reality is manifested instantly when the conditioned mind is dissipated and the experiencer is integrated into Universality.

One more reminder: the attachment to the accumulations of the physical world: material possessions or riches, knowledge baggage, titles, glory, fame etc. are obstacles, making it difficult to transcend the finite, relative world of vanities into the reality of beauty and inexhaustible pricelessness of the Sacred Boundlessness.

Awakening and Listening

Here is what Life asks of us, from birth until death:
A permanent attentiveness of our overflowing
                              thinking process;
Conditioned by time, by relative energies,
It dominates our whole being.

All conflictual states and all the misery in our life
Appear as effects of this unreal contact
Between newness – alive and active – and the old formulas
Recorded in the past, completely outdated in the now.

Therefore, Attentive to the gate of the mind, as thoughts
                                        barge in,
Listening in utter innocence – everything… absolutely
                                        everything melts,
In the pause between moments, we encounter a different
                                        Energy,
Untouched by time – Absolute Purity – radiating harmony.

We do not intervene in any way, we allow It to lead us,
Only in this manner do we encounter the freshness of Life!
We have no center, no bounds – melting into Infinity,
We live moments of happiness – each human being's
                                        destiny.

Awakening is a meditation taking place in the present,
In innocent silence – we just watch and listen, attentively,
To all the reactions that surface – as a response to Life's
                                        challenges;
Such simplicity ends all pain.

Wakefulness or awakening, a state in which the mind is
constantly illuminated, is required by Life Itself, in order
to understand the newness and freshness associated with
Its endless movement. Without this Light we can never
correctly encompass and comprehend the moments which

measure and refresh the Aliveness in Its eternal mobility.

This is what Life asks of us, from the moment of our birth until the moment we detach from the garment provided by this planet.

This is also the essence of the experience of "Self-knowing", which is neither a theory, nor a method, as it may appear at first glance.

By neglecting this imperative of Life, we are in danger of being attracted, according to our conditioning, either into an outdated past – in the present only hollow images – or into a fictitious and uncertain future.

Because of this unconscious trip to "yesterday" or "tomorrow", we miss the reality and beauty of Life in the eternal present. Furthermore, the past and the future can only provide an imaginary existence, frequently accompanied by depression. The whole sorrow and misery of life and its conflictual states are created by the misguided encounter between the new, active and constantly present man and the shadows of the past, as obsolete forms.

Therefore, let us always be attentive to the gate of the mind, through which thoughts, images, desires, feelings barge in, in the chaotic movement created by their fragmentary energies. By watching and listening to these unwanted apparitions, in innocence – they disappear and melt, as well as their intrinsic energies. In the silence or peace that ensues naturally, we encounter a different Energy – Absolute Purity – beyond time – radiating immense clarity and harmony. From now on we let ourselves be led by this Pure Energy and, without intervening in any way, It unites us with the freshness of Life.

From that fortunate moment, we are beyond form and we have no bounds. We fully live the transcendence of being in perfect union with the absolute Truth. We are "One" with Divinity and we know – through a direct experience – Love and Happiness.

This state of wakefulness or awakening is a state of meditation, taking place in the present; in humble silence, we simply listen and watch – with an all-encompassing Attention – all the reactions of the mind which appear in the encounter with the permanent challenges coming either from the external world or from the interior of our being.

The holy simplicity of this encounter with ourselves ends all confusion, frustration, fear and chaos, existent both at the level of man-"ego" or personality, as well as at the level of the whole humankind.

The Last Surprise

In the following account I will try to describe the shattering of the "ego" or the first Liberation. This phenomenon was not a goal to be pursued. It appeared as an absolute surprise and it happened at night, during sleep.

I was fifty-five years old. One morning, in the month of August, when I woke up from sleep – to my surprise – I noticed that, psychologically, I was functioning differently from the night before. My thinking and my whole being were functioning as a Whole, as a monolith. Each movement, as well as everything that I was hearing or seeing were encountered in perfect simplicity. A contained Joy and an Energy I had never experienced before created a simple state of "being", present to present.

The complete surprise temporarily prevented me from being able to define the phenomenon or to name it, based on what I knew. On my way to work, I encountered everything and everyone in a different way. People, things, animals – without any discrimination – were regarded with an all-encompassing perception. The serenity of the mind and clarity defined me as a blessing.

After a couple of hours, the curious thinking process started to ask itself questions about the mysterious phenomenon. Finally, I understood that this was the Liberation from the shackles of the "ego". From then on, subjective thinking lost its energy; it became futile. The religious faith I had treasured with fanaticism completely detached from me, without any form of intervention on my part. After experiencing this surprise phenomenon, I now deem faith as meaningless. The simplicity and the lucidity of the mind are my constant companions, integrating me into the alive and active present.

All psychological problems are spontaneously dissipated through a simple contact with the rays of all-encompassing, lucid Attention, my constant companion.

Nagged by a firm, profound and persistent inner impulse, I started to write about "Self-knowing". In less than a year and a half I wrote three hundred poems. After a sixteen-year break, from the same impulse I mentioned earlier, I started writing again, in poems and prose.

I ask myself: Why do I write? The answer and the explanation appear spontaneously. Everything I do, write or describe is in order to correctly inform my fellow beings interested in such a phenomenon, which can be experienced by any individual. Thanks to "Self-knowing", any person who practices this experience can simply dissolve all the tensional states which damage one's health, leading to an untimely death.

Such a phenomenon cannot be sought, wanted or imagined as an ideal or goal to fulfill. Any attempt – performed by the "ego" – in order to reach this state is nothing but an obstacle and it only further delays its appearance. Any form of ideal is nothing but an egoic creation, determined by a thought which creates vanity, arrogance and pride. Furthermore, the "ego" is a limited structure, confined by time-space and unable to surpass its own limits.

In spite of all these functional deficiencies of the human spirit, the state of Liberation nevertheless occurred, without pursuing it in any shape or form. A while before, discontent with everything I was practicing with the purpose of ennoblement of the soul, I realized that any changes performed through will, effort or imagination were merely superficial.

After this realization, I resorted to another practice, namely: encountering the reactions of the mind by simply watching and listening to them, without pursuing any ideal or goal. From the very beginning, I discovered that by simply coming into contact with the reactions of the mind, they are dissipated, as well as the energies which create them. As these energies are progressively eliminated, the egoic structure loses its authority.

Let us explain this experiment in another way: Life, in Its constant movement, demands our full attention. By naturally following this requirement, without any involvement from the "ego", I was preparing – without being aware of this – the act of Liberation.

I would like to add further details regarding this encounter with Life, practiced during the last days before the Liberation phenomenon occurred: I was simply listening to the noise of the street, day and night, until the moment I fell asleep. It is a simple listening, in which thinking does not intervene in any way. When there was no noise, I was simply listening to the silence and melting with it.

When practicing "Self-knowing" – as I mentioned earlier – if, while listening, a thought, a desire, an image or a feeling appears, what do we need to do? A very simple thing: just point your whole Attention towards this undesirable intruder. Let the noise pass through you, without making any analyses or assessments regarding its source. We will proceed in the same manner when using an all-encompassing, all-inclusive watchfulness. We simply watch and see things and human beings, and we become one with them.

This passiveness of the mind is imposed, as I mentioned

earlier, by Life itself, in order to correctly understand It. With each encounter, the stronghold of the "ego" is weakened and the energies which sustain its time-space existence are dissipated.

Fear

When we function as "ego", as fragmentation,
We constantly live in fear;
It is always connected to a fact, to an event,
Or created by imagination.

Fear never exists as an independent state,
From birth until death, it is our constant companion;
Through paralyzing impulses, it anguishes
                    the whole being,
Whether it has real or imaginary causes.

Under the rule of fear, man makes wrong decisions,
Losing clarity;
Our physical body pays the difficult price
For its effects, whether we want this or not.

The brain, heart and stomach are directly traumatized,
Millions of cells are affected;
The shocks caused by fear lead to an untimely death,
We create our own diseases, by ignoring reality.

Fear is a psychological disease which must be treated.
Do not postpone! Engage your whole being,
For it is not easy. Absolute healing ensues
When the experiencer attains the wondrous integration.

The moment it appears, we are the fear,
The "ego" appears in the next moment,
As a distinct observer of this feeling;
There is constant conflict between fear and
                                    the fearful person.

We want to be other than what we are: this creates
                                          separation
From the reality of fear, as a true, concrete fact.
Can we see all this, in a perfect light,
Without intermediaries – through a direct contact?

The encounter with "what is" and "what appears",
                                    in total simplicity,
Frees the being from his chains;
When we encounter fear in this manner, it immediately
                                          disappears,
In the empty space, we experience moments of liberation.

As a whole being – Pure Energy
Dissipates everything it encounters, in any circumstance;
Equilibrium, harmony, peace, inner order,
Reveal – moment to moment – the eternal Liberation.

Fear is a profound state of turmoil and unrest, triggered by a real or an imaginary danger. This emotion is closely connected to our existence as "ego", in other words, a fragmentary creation of the knowing mind.

Fear does not exist as an independent state, for it is always connected to a fact, an event or a desire.

From the moment we are born until the moment we pass into the beyond, we will always encounter fear as paralyzing impulses which affect our whole being, either based on a real motivation or purely imaginary. Under the impulse of fear we take rash decisions, or we are simply paralyzed with fear. Its effects – in both cases – can only be detrimental. Our physical body is under a lot of strain when we are overwhelmed by its impulses. The brain, heart and stomach are directly traumatized. Similarly, millions of cells in the nervous system are affected. In time, through repetition, the shocks of fear will eventually result in various diseases, leading to a premature death.

Psychologically, fear itself is a disease which needs to be treated in all earnestness. Let us not postpone the treatment and start this very moment.

Practically, we are the fear, the very moment it arises. Nevertheless, in the next moment the "ego" also appears, as a separate observer of the fear phenomenon. From now on, there is an inherent conflict between fear and the fearful entity, the "ego". We are something and we want to become something else. In this manner, we separate ourselves from fear as a real, true fact.

Can we see all these in the light of lucid and impersonal Attention?

A simple encounter with "what is" – as a reaction of the mind – makes it disappear; the "psychological void" leads to the state of liberation. From that moment on, as united beings in a State of Pure Consciousness, everything we encounter is dissipated.

The inner harmony, peace of the soul, aloneness – attained in this manner – reveal – moment by moment – the state of liberation.

The Evolution of the Planet

Nowhere in the universe is there fixedness,
Absolute stillness as a concrete reality.
On the contrary! In the Immense Boundlessness
Everything – seen or unseen – is in eternal movement.

Movement is change, permanent renewal,
From one moment to another – perpetual evolution;
All that was is left behind and discarded,
The foolish "ego" – created from the old.

It becomes arrogant, in thought and reason,
Its intellectual ability – outdated and obsolete –
Cannot comprehend the renewing Beauty
Intrinsic to the flow of Life, as a constant blessing.

Just as we were once incarnated as a human being,
Evolving in time, towards maturity,
Planet Earth also evolves,
Her journey spans billions of years.

From her frail beginnings, to her present state,
Through her real nature, she provides us with
All we need in order to live well:
Light, air, water, as well as food.

Scientists affirm that the planet is still young and
                                        prosperous,
All we request, she gives us abundantly.
In exchange, how do we treat her? Do we respect her ecology?
The planet is a living being – we need to take care of her!

Out of ignorance and selfish small-minded agendas,
We have become the enemies of the planet; every day,
The chemical industry, pesticides, herbicides –
                              thrown at random,
Ever-increasing exhaust fumes from cars and factories.

Let us bring awareness to other human mistakes,
Damaging the environment, through artificial actions:
Reckless deforestation, damaging all forms of vegetation
Which support the climate of the planet, creating serious
imbalance.

The air is increasingly polluted, the desert grows,
The human being is the only cause for this destruction;
We are also endowed with sophisticated weapons,
Able to destroy life in its totality.

The evolution of the planet, and of Life in general,
Depends on her master – a human being functioning as one;
Love and Wisdom, his essential characteristics,
Able to guide him to spiritual fulfillment.

In the whole Universe, in the immensity of all forms which make up Its content, there is no fixedness or frozenness. Eternal movement is in close connection with change or evolution, from gross states to more subtle states of being.

As far as the human being is concerned, each movement realized in unfolding moments is always new and renewing itself in the eternal process of evolution.

Everything that appears on the mirror of consciousness is a residue which needs to be discarded and left behind – for it is nothing but residual matter, creating and maintaining the false "self". Within this limited structure, the mind or the intellect assumes psychological importance and makes it impossible to perceive the Beauty of Life in its perpetual freshness. This permanent flow of Aliveness in its unfoldment is a true blessing, bestowed by the Divine on all beings, as help in their spiritual evolution towards more and more subtle existential forms.

Just as we human beings evolve, similarly Planet Earth is in a continuous process of evolution. From her beginnings as an embryo – billions of years ago – she attained the form of today; she generously provides optimal conditions of existence and development for an infinite number of living forms, in a constant evolution. The planet absolutely provides us with everything we need: air, water, light and food. This planet is still young – as scientists affirm – and she abundantly satisfies all our needs for development.

The question each individual needs to ask himself is: What is our behavior towards her? Do we respect her ecologically? The Planet is, as we mentioned earlier, a living being. Billions of years ago, she had an embryonic beginning, then a stage of development and, just like human beings, one day she will perish. Her health depends, to a great extent, on our behavior and the care we give her.

Yet, what do we see? Through savage deforestation, the forests – the true lungs of the planet – which provide us with the oxygen indispensable for life have been replaced with immense deserts; the extent of the desert areas should concern us. The chemical industry, with its various herbicides, pesticides, thrown at random; the exhaust fumes expelled by factory chimneys and the increasing number of cars pollute the air which is so necessary to our health. We also need to remind ourselves of the great danger threatening the health of the planet and of man in general: the nuclear experiments and increasing number of nuclear weapons, able to destroy life on this planet many times over.

The health and moral evolution of our planet, as well as that of her inhabitants, depends on each individual. We become aware of this responsibility and we totally accept it only when we function as a Whole, in perfect Oneness with the Unique Reality or God. "Self-knowing" represents the direct Path, with beneficial consequences, easy to perceive the very moment we correctly put it into practice.

Light Is Joy

When consciousness is illuminated by the flame-Attention,
This illumination dissipates all that is disharmony;
The "ego", created by time, full of worries and
                                        attachments,
Chains and enslaves our life with its egocentrism.

Light is eternally one with Joy,
Through It, Love pulsates; we live in a child-like wonder,
The purity of the soul that we had in the beginning,
In the clarity of the mind, we live as a newly-born.

There is nothing else to accomplish! Psychologically, this is
                                        not an action
Such as any directed efforts we perform on the
                                        physical plane.
Spiritually, we just encounter "what is",
Without any goals or aspirations.

This simple encounter with silence detaches us from
                                              all that was,
For the past and the future cannot coexist with the present;
The future is also old, just a hollow projection,
They are both imaginary, worthless.

Only the present offers you the joy of "being",
In silence, we just watch "what is", without desires or will.
In the moment, Eternity with Its renewing effects
Transforms our limited mind and it becomes creative.

Within each human being – as well as within each living being – a Primordial Light exists; It never changes Its clarity or Its ability to permeate all things. Without this Light we would be unable to understand ourselves or the Reality of Life in Its permanent movement. In Its absence, no authentic relationships can exist between human beings or with nature in general.

Although this Light is within us, awaiting for us to use It, nevertheless the path to the Light is so arduous! Why is it so difficult to discover it?

We have set foot on the Moon and we want to reach the soil of the planet Mars, yet we cannot cross this infinitesimal distance between our surface consciousness and the inexhaustible Source of Light in the depth of our being?!

Impersonal and lucid Attention is the medium for this attainment. This Attention is triggered spontaneously by the impressions coming from the external world, as well as from our inner being.

Let us not confuse it with the relative attention directed by thinking and sustained by will – fragmentary and self-seeking.

The impersonal, all-encompassing Attention is the everlasting light within each of us, without any exception, uniting us as one. With the help of this Light-Attention, we will encounter the disorder within us, created by the dysfunctional structure of the "ego".

When this Light appears, all confusion, sorrow, fears, attachments, suffering, greed etc. instantly disappear and we encounter the Peace of the soul and an immense Light accompanied by Joy – in this state, creative Love appears.

In this blissful state, we are spiritual Purity – Pure Consciousness or a newly-born Man. The simplicity of silence detaches us from all the ancestral residues, outdated and useless in the encounter with the perpetually fresh newness of Life in its eternal movement.

Similarly, the future is also meaningless, for it is also the past projected into the tomorrow as a hollow image.

Both Light and the Joy that accompanies it are encountered by melting in a state of "being" or Pure Consciousness. Therefore, in total and humble silence, we simply watch and listen to "what is" or what appears on the screen of the mind. That and nothing else!

In that moment of freedom and inner aloneness, we encounter Eternity; it ennobles and radically changes the whole mind, as it becomes creative.

Life and Death

Life, the Aliveness in movement, without beginning or
end,
Has Its Source in Eternity, with its whole content.
It has always existed and it will always be, eternally,
We can call it any way we like – or we can call it God.

It wasn't created by anyone, Existent through Itself,
Absolute Purity and perpetual freshness
In permanent movement, renewing itself each moment,
Each moment is unique. It never repeats itself!

Being constant movement, It is also perpetual change,
Perfection in Itself, always evolving
Towards deeper meanings, following a natural impulse
Given by Divinity.

It is within us – human beings – as a "luminous Dot",
Advising and guiding us, in a harmonious way,
We encounter It practically and we truly know It
When we function as a whole – in a state of Love.

This Divine Spark has been incarnated in thousands
                                        of bodies,
According to the divine order,
As an intrinsic experience of universal dimensions,
Greatness trapped in ideal forms.

***

Finally, the Aliveness returns to the Divine Alive Whole,
To Its Home – the Immense Sublime Realm.
This Aliveness, as a Spark, is within each of us,
In all of us It is equally manifest.

***

Death is just a word – meaningless,
Devoid of any sense, truth or reality;
For in everything that exists, in the whole Universe,
The Aliveness reigns everywhere, in an absolute, real way.

Life pervades everything: human beings, animals, plants,
In the mineral realm, also in a stone or a rock.
The outer layer is just an external piece of clothing,
It disintegrates when it can no longer be used.

That which we call death is nothing but the
                                immortal Aliveness
Leaving Its ephemeral garment when it becomes damaged,
Moving into another world – a more subtle dimension
With multiple qualities and a perfect understanding.

Life – by Its very nature, all-encompassing Energy in eternal movement – has no beginning and It will never have an end, because Its Source lies in Eternity and, through Its very content, It will continue to exist endlessly. During the historical past of our planet, different symbols have been used to express It: Cosmic Energy, Absolute Truth, God. It was not created by anyone and It exists only through Itself as Absolute Purity and freshness from one moment to another. Its permanent movement, in renewing moments, assures Its continuous evolution, as Perfection perfecting itself in Its eternal mobility.

This Life, existent in All and Everything, is also found within each human being, as a "luminous Dot" or a Sparkle called Soul or Spirit. The moment we are conscious of Its presence within us, we become one with It, manifesting ourselves as disinterested and all-encompassing Love.

Throughout Its long journey, this Spark has been incarnated in a long series of bodies within the physical Universe, until It reached the present level of evolution as a human being. This Process of evolution in association with matter will continue, as It follows the path of return Home, to the Source It originated from: the Body of the Creative Divine.

As far as death is concerned, deemed to be the end of Life, this word is devoid of content and reality. Nowhere in the Universe is there any death, as a state of fixedness. The Aliveness is present everywhere, even in so-called still life, namely the mineral realm. We need to mention, nevertheless, that all the external layers which make up the cloak of the various bodies disintegrate, when they are unable to continue the duality in the physical Universe.

That which we call death is nothing but the immortal Aliveness simply leaving Its bodily clothing, when it is degraded because of old age or some sort of accident. After this detachment, the Soul travels to another dimension, more subtle, with multiple possibilities of comprehension and action.

In this context, let us be reminded of another frequent occurrence during the death of a person. The loved ones, in fact, do not cry for the departed, but rather they cry for themselves, because they lose certain advantages they had from the presence of the deceased. We need to be aware of this phenomenon as well, in our encounter with ourselves, in such circumstance.

The Moment

The moment is the meeting point with Life in Its
                                    eternal movement,
In its essence – a mystery – continuously renewing itself;
Therefore, we also need to be newness,
Let the "ego" be silent, be just humble simplicity!

We let go of the lived moment, welcoming the next
                                    moment,
Only thus we embrace Life in its unfoldment;
Free when we encounter the moment, free when it leaves,
Through our freedom we encounter Love.

The moment is Eternity, a pause between thoughts,
In this "vacuum", we expand into Infinity;
The moment and freedom are inseparable,
We need to give them their due, so we can encounter
                                        Reality.

Only the simplicity of the mind, in total silence,
Can encompass the moment and integrate into Being;
We are awakened – a state of Enlightenment,
A state we have been searching for millennia, through
                                various practices.

Time, accompanying the Aliveness in movement, comes
from eternity and flows towards the same eternity. Life, as
well as time, has no beginning and no end. The present
moment represents a mere flash on the trajectory of this
eternal movement.

Always enveloped in the cloak of mystery, this eternal
moment cannot be foreseen or intuited by the knowing
mind. Its lightning-like movement is eternal newness, as
well as uniqueness. Therefore, no two moments are alike;
each second is strictly unique.

Our encounter with the Reality of Life is performed
through a direct contact with each moment. As we have
shown earlier, Its very essence is newness, and we need to
greet It with a similar mind, always fresh from one
moment to another.

Our whole memorial past needs to be silent, as well as
our ancestral mind, conditioned by its history. Only a
humble, fresh, completely free mind, uncontaminated by
previous knowledge, can encounter the mystery of Life as
ever-renewing moments unfolding eternally. Just as free,

we will welcome the incoming moments in their eternal flow. Only in this circumstance can we encounter true Love, through a direct experience, and transcend from the finite world into Boundlessness.

This "psychological void", occurring spontaneously in the fleeting moment, enables us to expand to Infinity. In that very moment, new brain cells start to function, able to comprehend and encompass the newness and surprise provided by the moment.

Therefore, the simplicity of the mind, provided by its humble silence, opens the pathless path towards the integration of our being, simultaneously melting into Universality. Let us also mention that this spiritual state is what the whole of humanity has been aspiring to for thousands and thousands of years, whether consciously or unconsciously. All the searches have remained mere and hopeless ideals, because they were based on methods, concepts, faiths and practices which, by their very nature, are completely erroneous and unable to create a real transformation within our being.

Duality

Creation and creator, two different aspects, separated
by thought,
Matter and idea, man and Divinity,
Thought and the thinker, fear and the fearful entity
Are just a few revealing examples.

Why is there separation in the living moment?
How does the Whole divide itself, in this encounter?
I am creation, fear, thought, I am Divinity and matter,
When I am just "being", in utter simplicity.

This "something" which separates is the fictitious "ego",
Through obsessive impulses, it creates separation.
Conflict is born out of dualism, people live in enmity,
Because they don't know their own being.

When I observe the desire, thought, the sentimental
                                    impulse,
I am one with them, in the now,
There is no separation – I define myself as unity,
In this state, I am Love and I love.

It is only when duality vanishes that harmony ensues,
Body and mind as one, opening to the eternal spheres.
We encounter Reality; through It, we become happy,
We find the meaning of life, united with the moment.

What is duality? In which circumstances do we encounter
it? What effects does it have on our daily existence?
    Duality is the co-existence of two separate and opposite
principles or elements. It appears within the limited
structure of the "ego" and its effects are intrinsically
connected to its dysfunctional and subjective structure.
Here are a few examples: creation – creator, fear – fearful
entity, matter – spirit, man – Divinity, thought – thinker. All
these are creations of thinking, as opposite aspects,

according to the assessment of the conditioned mind of the man prisoner of time-space.

Why, as we experience the moment, is the Whole divided?

When the human being, as a united structure, encounters the wholeness of Life, he is nothing but: creation, matter, man, fear – as facts. All of these are and will remain as such: "what is" – if we live in a state of simplicity – "being" in the present moment.

In all these examples, the "ego" is the only one guilty of introducing the opposite; by functioning through obsessive impulses, it creates duality.

Because of these fictitious creations, contradictions and conflicts appear; human beings become enemies because of this erroneous way of functioning.

What happens if we simply watch the thought, desire, fear etc. as they appear?

We will discover that we are all these and, in fact, they define the reality of our being in that very moment, as thought, desire, fear. By encountering them in this manner, they disappear; in the "psychological emptiness" that ensues, our being is extended into Infinity and we encounter Love; we are Love, and not a separate entity who loves.

It is only when the duality within us disappears that we will know harmony and the equilibrium of the soul, transcending us into the spheres of Eternity. In this direct encounter – by directly experiencing reality – we discover the meaning of life and unconditional, undesired, unmotivated Happiness.

Attention

Attention is light, harmony – infinite purity,
It has no center and no limits – a boundless energy;
Through it, the Sacred mirrors its immortality,
Only in a state of attention, Love appears.

A sacred, unique instrument for our evolution,
Dissipating the "ego" and its hideous bondage;
Without it, it is impossible to encounter what is real,
It dissolves the past, creating an integral being.

The constant challenges of Life in Its movement
Are wonderful opportunities to test this instrument;
Attentive to all impulses – the mind is completely mute
                                                          and silent,
In the emptiness that ensues, the Sublime defines us.

Creating sparkling flashes in the darkness of life,
Perfectly enlightened, the mind comprehends and acts
Universally, through direct experience,
Only through Attention – our Existence is pure.

Enlightenment, an Eternal Beginning

The blissful man, spiritually transformed,
Lives as an integrated man, perpetually,
Completely detached from the worldly and its duality,
He is an eternal beginning, in union with the moment.

The newness, the freshness of the moment –
                                    an Infinite Energy
Nourishes him, it gives him Life, in perfect form;
One with Enlightenment, he is dead to the past,
Reborn, he is unlike anything in this world.

Enlightenment in itself is the end of ignorance,
Like a ray of light, it dissipates the darkness;
When it starts, it had no end...
Thus the human being knows his own Reality.

Living beyond mind – a hallowing Purity,
Any separation vanishes – all is one;
Beauty, Kindness, boundless Happiness
And creative Love are experienced, beyond images.

***

The mind was created by time, it thinks in symbols,
Through beliefs and concepts, with subjective meanings,
It has created the world of today, full of conflicts and
                                        contradictions,
Constantly increasing, with its roots in tradition.

This troubled climate – through simple enlightenment –
Is instantly dissipated, for it is just an illusory shadow,
An accumulation of symbols and past experiences,
Meaningless in the eternal, alive and active present.

An enlightened man lives, moves and acts
From one moment to another, without imagining anything
Or using his mind, in any form,
For it is always the old and its bondage.

Encountering Reality, without mental projections,
Through a direct union and total humbleness;
Truly living in the moment and acting with the moment,
                                        as totality,
The moment arrives and acts spontaneously,
                        in its wholeness.

The Psychological Void

The void is a total vacuum, an emptiness,
Empty of substance, of any material content;
When knowledge is silent,
The mind is empty.

This emptiness affirms itself, by itself,
Between one word and another, in conversation;
It is a certain and natural inherent reality,
It cannot be anticipated or created.

The void can also be encountered in the thought process,
In silent speech;
In the space between thoughts or words,
Emptiness is constantly manifest.

No matter how fast we think or speak,
An intermittent "void" appears.
What happens, what do we feel when we become one
                                             with it?
Is this encounter possible? Try it!

Melting with it, in simplicity – can we notice that the mind
disappears?
In this union, a transformation occurs:
We become Immensity – a great joy envelops us,
We are a state of "being" – Pure Consciousness and Love.

This "void" contains both the finite and the Infinite,
It is, in fact, also within us
In the stillness of the mind,
Melting with the emptiness between thoughts and words.

In "Self-knowing", this "void" appears,
In every circumstance,
Encountering Life, in Its eternal movement,
Absolute freshness, newness each moment.

Dominated by the body, the senses and the knowing mind,
We cannot perceive Life, nor the immortal Being;
We need to become unity and dispel the powerlessness,
By going beyond the false, we eliminate the ignorance.

We point our lucid Attention to the mental space:
Thoughts, desires and feelings – the emotional structure,
When illuminated, it is spontaneously dissipated
and disappears,
In the "emptiness" that ensues, we are completely free.

In this climate of peace, holy transformations occur,
The Sacred, by its simple presence, cleanses and dispels
                              what we have accumulated,
Applying this persistently and diligently finally leads to
                                    Enlightenment,
When the blissful person loses his possessive "self".

Words Are Shadows

A shadow is not an object in itself,
But only a projection of something real;
Similarly, the word is only a mental projection
Attempting to express a true reality.

When we listen to words, the intellect comes into play,
Truth – as essence – is instantly distorted;
This is where all contradictions and conflicts originate,
People fight one another over reckless opinions.

This is an invitation to go beyond the thought-word,
And encounter Reality, in its Sacred Unfoldment;
Attentive with all our feeling – our whole being in
                              the present,
We discover the meaning of life – independent from
                              the past.

Truth reveals itself, by itself, in the psychological void,
The passiveness of the mind creates Sacred Action;
We will use words, in certain circumstances,
Offering explanations to those who request them.

Break Your Cup

When the cup of the "ego" is full and the mind is busy,
We cannot encounter life – the being is a prisoner.
The cup must be emptied
In the "psychological void".

Only such a mind becomes universal,
Expanding into Infinity, beyond all conflicts;
Only thus can we perceive all that comes in the moment,
As a divine gift, leading us to Divinity.

Quickly, break your cup! Let all its contents disappear!
No preferences for what was in the past.
We surrender, totally, to life in its unfoldment,
The Absolute envelops us spontaneously.

You cannot attain this wise shattering
Through will, effort, analyses, self-improvement,
Faiths, prayers or repeating mantras;
Only through humble silence.

Love Is Always in the Present

When we encounter Love – we are in communion with It,
Neither past, nor future participate in this meeting,
Based on memory or fictitious anticipation,
Purpose, goal, ideal or imagination.

Let us investigate deeper;
We can never remember a dead love,
Nor can we project it onto what might be,
In an uncertain future.

In Love, there is no "other" – for it is not duality,
Just simple being: only Love, in the "now" – Reality.
It is an all-encompassing, all-inclusive phenomenon,
Revealing itself by itself, inside and outside ourselves.

Such encounters continuously transform
The individual programmed by time and knowledge;
Empty words, hollow images define his behavior,
A fearful being, ruled by despair.

Each moment of Love cleanses and dissipates
The selfish structure which defines the individual,
In everything he thinks, says or does;
A millennial conditioning, inherited through education.

On that happy day, the egocentric shell,
Its energies are constantly dissipated...
Suddenly, it collapses! The event is a total surprise,
It cannot be wanted or desired, in any shape or form.

This spontaneous phenomenon is called Enlightenment.
Our mentality is transformed, without effort or will;
Life is understood differently, free from beliefs or concepts,
A direct contact with Divinity.

Absorbed into the Infinite, the human being becomes
                                            Infinite!
The old man disappears! The New – a humble
                              "Emptiness",
A state of Pure Consciousness. There is no "I", no thinking,
The state of "being" is Sacred in its unfoldment.

About the Author

Ilie Cioara was an enlightened mystic who lived in Bucharest, Eastern Europe. His writings in 16 books describe the experience of meditation and enlightenment, as well as the practice of Self-knowing using all-encompassing Attention. Like Ramana Maharshi, Krishnamurti, Eckhart Tolle, his is a simple message of discovering our inner divine nature through the silence of the mind.

The author's description of enlightenment, in his own words:

I was 55 years old. One morning, waking up from my sleep, I noticed that, psychologically, I was functioning differently from the night before. The mind had lost its usual turmoil. In a state of serenity I had never felt before, I was functioning in perfect communion with my whole somatic structure.

Only after a couple of hours I realized what had happened to me, without pursuing this "something" as an ideal to accomplish. I was, to use a simile, in the situation of a man blind from birth, who had just gained his sight after undergoing surgery. Everything around me was as new. I had an overall perspective on things. A silent mind allows the senses to perceive things as they are.

Through silence, the mind in its totality had become an immense mirror in which the outside world was reflected. And the world I was perceiving directly through my senses revealed its own reality to me. My fellow beings, close friends or complete strangers, were being regarded indiscriminately, with a feeling of love I had never felt before.

If any reaction of the mind surfaced, it disappeared immediately in contact with the sparkle of impersonal Attention. A state of quiet and all-encompassing joy characterized me in all circumstances, whether pleasant or painful. My behavior was that of a simple witness, perfectly aware of what was happening around me, without affecting my all-encompassing state of peace.

The State of the Sublime is, of course, difficult to describe, but not impossible to experience by someone who authentically practices awareness. In order to communicate it, a simple and direct language is used, which is not filtered through reason, because the "ego", with its subjective perception, is no longer there. To put it this way: the psychological emptiness is the one who lives the present moment, expresses this encounter into words and still remains present and available to the next moment.

Also Available

Ilie Cioara

The Silence of the Mind

***

The Wondrous Journey Into the Depth of Our Being

***

Life Is Eternal Newness

Published by O-Books
www.o-books.com

BOOKS

O is a symbol of the world, of oneness and unity. In different cultures it also means the "eye," symbolizing knowledge and insight. We aim to publish books that are accessible, constructive and that challenge accepted opinion, both that of academia and the "moral majority."

Our books are available in all good English language bookstores worldwide. If you don't see the book on the shelves ask the bookstore to order it for you, quoting the ISBN number and title. Alternatively you can order online (all major online retail sites carry our titles) or contact the distributor in the relevant country, listed on the copyright page.

See our website www.o-books.net for a full list of over 500 titles, growing by 100 a year.

And tune in to myspiritradio.com for our book review radio show, hosted by June-Elleni Laine, where you can listen to the authors discussing their books.

mySpiritRadio